DROPPING THE HABIT

Marion Dante always knew, that as her mother's 'sin offering', she would be a nun. At the age of fourteen, she entered a convent . . . Years later, wrestling with doubts and misery, she embarked on the long and terrifying road to freedom. Like a caged bird she clung to her prison bars. Wearing a short skirt, ordering a cup of tea in a café, everyday conversation with a stranger, were mountains to climb. More frighteningly — if she dropped the habit, who then would she be? What would remain of Marion Dante if she broke out of her protective shell?

Marion Dante hails from Limerick but has lived in England since 1955 when there were signs on some doors saying 'No Blacks. No dogs. No Irish.' She started training to be a nun aged fourteen when she became an aspirant in Chertsey, Surrey. She was dispensed from her vows thirty-two years later in 1991 aged forty-seven. Ever since, she has been playing 'catch up'. She belongs to Camberley Writers' Circle and Book Club. She enjoys badminton, yoga, swimming, water aerobics, walking, guitar-playing, learning Italian, art and travelling. Having had breast cancer, Marion helps to raise funds for The Fountain Centre in The Royal Surrey Hospital. In 2004 she climbed Machu Picchu in Peru for this cause. As a retired teacher she is also engaged in a little home tutoring. Being single, she involves herself with her brother, two sisters and their extended family.

MARION DANTE

DROPPING
THE HABIT

Complete and Unabridged

ULVERSCROFT
Leicester

First published in the Republic of Ireland in 2007 by
Poolbeg Press Ltd.
Dublin

First Large Print Edition
published 2011
by arrangement with
Poolbeg Press Ltd.
Dublin

British Library CIP Data

Dante, Marion.
  Dropping the habit.
  1. Dante, Marion. 2. Ex-nuns- -Ireland- -Biography.
  3. Nuns- -Ireland- -Biography. 4. Ex-nuns- -
  England- -Biography. 5. Nuns- -England- -Biography.
  6. Large type books.
  I. Title
  271.9′7′092–dc22

  ISBN 978-1-4448-0887-2

Published by
F. A. Thorpe (Publishing)
Anstey, Leicestershire

Set by Words & Graphics Ltd.
Anstey, Leicestershire
Printed and bound in Great Britain by
T. J. International Ltd., Padstow, Cornwall

This book is printed on acid-free paper

Dedication

My parents Frank and Patricia Dante
(née Colivet) RIP and my brothers
Tim (RIP) and Desmond,
my sisters Patricia and Bernadette.

And to Saint John Bosco. Born in 1815
into a poor family in Becchi, Italy, he
dedicated his life to the education of
deprived young people, inspiring thousands of others to do the same. He was
indeed a great innovator who continues to
enthuse me to this day.

Acknowledgements

Particular thanks to my nephew Mark Stay for his help, support and encouragement.

Also to the members of both the Camberley & Chobham Writers' Circles: Peter Rolls, Margaret Cronin and Bill Erith to mention a few. Appreciation also to Alison Burke for her proof-reading. Healthwise, I have also received a great deal of support from Charlotte McDowell, Gail Maguire and Nicky Bracey at The Fountain Centre in The Royal Surrey Hospital, Guildford. Finally, how would I have coped without the friendship of Jackie Wetherell, Gill McCarraher, Zeta Ashforth and many others too numerous to list.

Acknowledgement and gratitude are due to the writer Bead Roberts who not only suggested the title of the book but launched me off on its production.

Sincere thanks also to Mrs Barbara Large MBE FRSA FUW, Founder-Director of the Annual Writers' Conference in the University of Winchester, for her support in the past, present and — it seems — future!

I am exceedingly grateful to Poolbeg Press.

Never in my wildest dreams did I imagine I would be accepted by such a renowned publishing house. I appreciate the Irish warmth and humanity that appears so laid back but underneath is thoroughly competent and inspiring and is so good to experience. If only it could be bottled and taken twice a day!

Special thanks to my editor Gaye Shortland — Gaye, you are tops for all your patience, thoroughness and expertise — I had no idea there was so much involved in editing and I am so grateful; to the wonderful Paula Campbell who makes a newcomer feel so relaxed, while at the same time is a mile ahead — planning strategy and spurring on her superb team; to Kieran Devlin, for all his help and advice; and to Lynda Laffan, Niamh Fitzgerald and David Prendergast.

In order to protect the identity of some of those involved in my story, I have not used their actual names in the course of this narrative. Some of the place names have also been changed.

Contents

Preface

What kind of God wanted me to be my mother's sin offering?

The dollops of guilt the Church plonked on my mother affected many lives. When I became conscious of this I wanted 'out' and I wrote to the Pope.

> 6, Moonshine Avenue
> Wimbledon
> London SW19 8PR
> 6th January 1991

Dear Pope John Paul II,

I, Marion Dante, want to be released from the vows I made on August 5th 1965 as a member of the Religious Order of Daughters of Mary Help of Christians (Salesian Sisters) founded by Saint John Bosco.

I have tried hard during the three years granted me to consider whether or not I

1

should renew my vows and have come to the conclusion that I find it too difficult to continue living in the convent. I therefore feel that, for the good of my health, I want to be released from the commitment of being a *Sister* in the *Salesian Order.*

Yours respectfully,
Marion Dante

I addressed the envelope to:

His Holiness Pope John II
The Vatican
Roma
ITALIA

The answer came, five months later, in the form of a document in Latin from the Congregatio Pro Institutis Vitae Consecratae, releasing me from my vows.

Dropping The Habit tells my journey of discovery and reveals whether or not I was able to cope after I was so easily let go.

' . . . *considerate la vostra semenza: fatti non foste a viver come bruti, ma per seguir virtute e conoscenza.*'

' . . . *consider your origin: you were not*

born to live like brutes but to follow
virtue and knowledge . . . '

DANTE: *Inferno Canto XXVI 1.118*

1

Sin Offering

Mammy was talking to herself again.

I was seated under the table on which she was scrubbing the potatoes and cutting up carrots and parsnips. She had an enamelled basin of water, a pot, a sharp knife and a small scrubbing brush. At first I thought she had forgotten all about me because she was snivelling and raising her voice and going on and on. Every now and then she'd bang on the table or thump the knife down hard, then the next minute her knees would sag and she'd crouch over the table as she let out a sort of a murmuring cry.

'Dear Jesus, why is this happening to me? Aren't I doing my level best to make up to you for what happened?' was what she said. Every time she thumped, though, she was calling out: 'The bitches, the lot of them! Why's everyone staring at me? Why won't they leave me alone? 'Tis a cruel way of punishing me!'

Our terraced stone cottage was one of ten that opened straight onto the street. It only had one small window in the front and the back one faced out on to a long narrow garden with a tumbledown wall at the bottom. The room was always dark and gloomy in the day-time and even worse at night with the one bulb struggling to light up the place.

Mammy's foot hit my back.

'Oh Jesus! I'm sorry, darling! I'd forgotten you down there listening to all my ranting and raving. You must be frozen on that concrete floor!'

She got up and hoisted me into her arms.

'This is not your fault. You know I'd never harm you. I'm sorry, darling! I love you! What am I doing to you?'

With that Mammy collapsed into an old armchair my Uncle Tim had given us. She cuddled me very tight — too tight — and told me all about when I was born.

'Now, my little treasure, let me tell you what a special little girl you are!'

Mammy's tears were spilling on to my face and however much she wiped me and her, both our faces were still wet on account of the fact that her hankie was soaking.

Now she made an effort and, controlling her tears, said, 'It was a Monday night at six o'clock when the Angelus Bells were ringing in the Franciscan church. You see, you were born in a nursing home just around the corner in Bedford Row. You could say that you were born in answer to prayer when the Angelus Bells were calling out to everyone to remember when Jesus Himself, Our Divine Lord, was born. Now isn't that a sign from Almighty God that you are special, born in answer to prayer? You belong to God.'

'I love you, Mammy. But why are you sad?'

Mammy burst into tears and slobbered all over me again. Then she pushed me a little bit away from her on her lap and between sobs she went on.

'Let me tell you more. We've called you after Our Lady. She's Jesus' mother just like I'm your mammy. We were going to christen you 'Mary' but there were too many girls being called 'Mary' so we put your name down as 'Marion'. So you are special.'

Then followed more hugs and kisses and a lot of wet patting before Mammy let me down and carried on putting the pots on the stove and waiting for Daddy to come home.

Every night she'd go out onto the street and look up in the direction of the Garda Barracks, straining her eyes to see any sign of him. We always knew Daddy though from far off because of his limp. He had an ulcerated leg on account of an injury he'd suffered playing rugby for Garryowen. Every night when he came home he would have to change the gauze and bandages and there would be a smell of ointment all round our house.

'Isn't she a little dote!'

I'd wrapped mum's long tweedy skirt around her legs and was peeping in and out and round and swinging and holding on to her. She smelt of that blue bottled Evening of Paris perfume she hid in her side of the wardrobe.

She was chatting to her friends Sheila and Norma.

I was so happy now that Mammy had stopped being so upset. I wondered if it was having my little brother that had caused it.

One day I'd overheard Granny Colivet telling Granddad: 'Having Oliver so soon after Marion was the ruination of Patsy. It's too much for her after letting herself down like that. She can't manage and what's more she's imagining that we're all against her. We had every reason to be cross but that's behind them now. She'll drive herself mad. She's having a breakdown, I tell you!'

And I hadn't set out to listen to what Daddy was saying to Mammy the other night but she kept repeating that everybody was watching and talking about her and Daddy kept saying, 'Patsy, please, will you believe me when I tell you that I really and truly love you, and your family and friends have forgiven us? Everything will be all right now, you'll see.'

Then there was the other time when Daddy came home from work and Mammy asked me to rock baby Oliver to sleep in his pram in the kitchen while she finished getting the dinner ready. Mammy had been crying and talking to herself again and I had tried to make her happy by hanging her cardigans and Daddy's shirts up in the wardrobe and putting the ware away and sweeping the floor. Now the steam from the stew nearly made me fall asleep. All of a sudden Daddy yelled as he rushed over and grabbed me up in his arms, 'For God's sake, Patsy, let the child alone! She's exhausted! Will you look what she's doing? She's rocking the bloody door handle!'

With that Mammy started to cry and they both cuddled me together. The very next day my case was packed and Daddy took me round to Granny and Granddad Colivet for a holiday.

It was while I was over with Granny that Daddy took me out for a ride on his bike. I had to take hold of the handlebars and he put his big strong, hairy hands over mine until we were out in the country and after we had stroked a big horse Daddy sat me down on a hillock next to him and explained.

'Mammy and me want you to play with Betty in the end house and we don't want you to be minding Oliver as much as you do. You love your little brother and that's only right but you're our little girl and we've been expecting too much of you. Do you understand?'

Mammy seemed like her old self when I came back home. She had stopped sobbing and she began to stop and talk to her friends again. In fact, today she was doing so much talking that she seemed to take no notice of me. I was jumping on and off the path and nearly bumped into Mammy's friend Sheila.

Sheila didn't seem to mind because she bent down to my size and said: 'Well, isn't she the image of Frank! Aren't you, darling? Sure you are! Haven't you got his lovely blue eyes and the hair and all? Well, now, aren't you a grand girl?'

'How old is she now, Patsy?' said Norma. 'She's fine and tall too. Coming up for six, did you say?'

'She'll be making her First Communion this June on the Feast of St Peter and Paul!' said Mammy proudly

'She's a grand girl, isn't she, Patsy?'

I smiled and looked up at Sheila and Norma and waited for Mam to say, like she always did, 'Tell them, Marion, what you're going to be when you grow up.'

'A nun,' I said and waited for all the attention that usually followed.

'Come here 'til I give you a hug! You're a credit to your mammy and daddy! Aren't they blessed with you?'

Then Sheila, like all the others who had been told before, patted me on the head and bent down so that her face was very close to mine and said those all-important words: 'Holy God must be very pleased with you. Aren't you the lucky one to have been chosen by God?'

Inside I felt so cosy and loved and delighted that I knew what I definitely would be when I grew bigger. I could imagine myself all dressed up in a long dress looking very important like the nuns who went to the Novena Devotions to Our Lady of Perpetual Succour up in The Fathers' Church. Everybody would know I had been a good girl.

★ ★ ★

'Your First Holy Communion is the most important thing to happen to you in your whole life. Jesus coming into your soul is what you have to remember.' This is what Mammy often said while I was being prepared for the big day.

In the Model School in Limerick my teacher had explained that the small wafer the priest would place on my tongue was the Sacred Body and Blood of Christ, the second person of the Blessed Trinity, God Almighty Himself.

'Am I going to get a First Holy Communion dress like Joan and Vera had when they made theirs?' I asked Mammy.

'What did I tell you about receiving Jesus? You mustn't think about what you're wearing. That will only distract you from what is important. Even if you only wear a flour sack, one that is washed and stitched to fit, it's Jesus coming into your soul that's important!'

Mammy took me to a shop down town and I fitted on a lovely white dress and a blue coat and a veil. It was the first time I had ever worn a veil. But she told me that I was trying these clothes on for another little girl who was the same size as me. Although I partly guessed that these clothes were for me, I was not certain until my granny unpacked my case on the night before the big day.

When Mammy told me that I would be

staying with my Granny Colivet and my aunts the night before my First Holy Communion I wondered why she was not going to get me ready. But she explained that Granny had a proper bath at her house and my aunties Evelyn and Mona would put rags in my hair so that I would have ringlets.

With my case packed, I stood waiting for the bus to pass our house in Ryans' Cottages, Rosbrien. Mam put her hand out to stop the bus and explained to the driver that my granny would be waiting by Fennessys' pub in the New Street. He agreed to put me off there.

The first thing Granny checked when we had walked the few yards from the bus stop to her house was that I was sure that I wouldn't wet the bed. Then I was fed and washed, rubbed in talcum powder and the rags put in my hair. There were night prayers to be said and another reminder that the next day would be a day I would remember until the day I died.

On the big day I was dressed in the frock that Mammy had said was for that other little girl who was the same size as me. My ringlets hung down over the collar of my new blue coat and my black patent shoes with a big buckle in front made me feel very swish.

Granny (or 'Aunty Mammy' as she insisted

we call her) had a bunch of white lilies ready for me to hold when I got into Granddad's black Prefect. We collected my friend Paula and Granddad drove us down to St Joseph's Church in O'Connell Street. My mam was waiting for us there and she told me that my Granddad Dante, who had died when I was two, had helped to build that church and it didn't matter that it was raining because I was going to receive Jesus and this was the most important day in my life. I had made my First Confession a week earlier so all my sins had been washed away by the Blood of Christ and I was pure as could be.

Then came the big moment. I was kneeling at the altar rails with all the other girls and boys in my class waiting for the priest to reach me. An altar boy held the golden communion plate under my chin and I lifted my head up, opened my mouth and stuck out my tongue so that the priest could put the Host on it. I could hear the voices of all who'd prepared me, telling me to remember that at the Consecration of the Mass, when the priest uttered the words, 'This is My Body and this is My Blood,' this wafer had become the Body and Blood of my Saviour Jesus Christ.

I did remember. I did manage to stop and really think about what was happening. I whispered: 'Welcome, Jesus! Welcome into my soul!'

Nothing else mattered. All the prayers and the singing of the hymns like 'Jesus, You Are Coming' and 'Soul of My Saviour' was lovely and I felt good and chosen and special. When we walked down the aisle and out onto the church steps to have a class photo taken, the sun was shining. I was kissed and then taken down the street to see my Granny Dante, who had not come to see me in church because she did not like going to big occasions — or so I was told.

Young as I was, I could sense that all was not well between the Dantes and the Colivets. Dad used to take my brother Oliver and me down to see Granny Dante after Mass on most Sundays. She called Oliver 'Tim' after his Uncle Tim but Dad used to wink and say that they had better keep to the name he was given at the christening. But, as he grew up, Oliver liked being called 'Tim' and gradually we all began to call him that. Mammy hardly ever came with us to visit Granny Dante and this added to my feeling that the Colivets did not approve of some things the Dantes did and vice versa but that for the sake of peace all was smoothed over.

After visiting my granny, we went down town to have a photo taken in a proper photographer's shop. Mammy took me into her friend's knitting shop in William Street and then into other stores and everybody gave me money. Mammy said that they really meant to give it to her but they gave it to me to give to her to help pay for my clothes and the photographers.

When we eventually got home I had to take off my First Holy Communion dress but I was allowed to keep on the gold chain and cross that my cousins Vera and Joan had given me. I soon wished I had not kept it on, though, because it must have slipped off when I went down the few hundred yards from my house to Hoares' to buy some sweets. Mammy tried not to be cross but nevertheless made me and my brother search up and down the road for hours. We never did find that cross and I wondered if God was disappointed at me for insisting that I be allowed to buy those sweets.

2

Traveller Woman

A Traveller woman told Mammy that if she crossed the sea she would live a long and happy life. I expect Mammy was delighted to hear that. Daddy's Aunty Nan had promised him the farm and the priests were warning everyone that it would be very difficult to hold onto their Faith if they went to live in England. But since no one seemed to be able to cure Mammy's unhappiness, she kept telling us that maybe we would have to travel to another country. In the meantime we all kept praying to have God's Holy Will made known to us.

'Isn't Aunt Mary getting deafer by the day?'

'Sure, doesn't deafness run in the Colivet family? Annie's nearly as deaf as her. The two of them make a fine pair, one shouting louder than the other!'

I knew what my parents were talking about because every time I was either going to or coming from the Redemptorist Church (known as 'The Fathers' Church' or simply

'The Fathers''), both my granddad's sisters would say a very loud 'hallo' to me.

'Good girl you are, Marion!' one or the other of them would shout. 'If you keep going to Holy Mass you'll learn all the responses and, what's more, on account of it being in Latin, when you get big and travel, wherever you go to in the world you'll be able to take part in this Holy Sacrifice of the Mass. It's the same everywhere!'

I'd smile and everybody would look at us and then I'd go in and find a place near the pulpit so I could see the altar too. There was lots of singing of hymns and reciting of prayers from a blue Novena of Perpetual Succour Prayer Book. At first, when the priest in the pulpit was dressed in a black soutane, a white surplice and a stole, there were only a few lights on but as it got nearer to the start of the Mass an altar boy came out to light the bigger candles on the high altar. Then the smells of the candles mingled with the incense in the thurible. A kind of heavenly mist came over the whole church and everybody. The altar boys had red soutanes under their while frilly surplices and carried lit candles in the procession from the sacristy, up the aisle and then to the altar. The swell of the organ accompanied the solemn voices of the congregation and it was all very grand

and made me feel as though I was ready for Heaven.

When we all sat down for the sermon the priest nearly always reminded us that there would be special people there in the congregation that Jesus was calling to follow Him.

"Go ye therefore, and teach all nations, baptising them in the name of the Father and of the Son and of Holy Ghost. Teaching them to observe all things whatsoever I have commanded you: and, lo, I am with you always, even to the end of the world. Amen." After quoting from Saint Matthew's Gospel the priest would explain: 'There will be three or four or maybe more of you who will hear God calling you to go and spread His Gospel, assured that the Holy Ghost, the third Person of the Holy Trinity, will be with you. It's a privilege to be called to be one of the chosen few, to help in saving the souls of those waiting and longing to hear the Word of God. As priests and nuns you may be sent out to darkest Africa or India or even to faraway South America to rescue black babies and tell their parents the message of salvation. We need priests and nuns to proclaim the Word of God and His power of Redemption to the four corners of the world. Remember how Jesus called his first two apostles to leave all

and follow Him: '*Now as Jesus was walking by the Sea of Galilee, He saw two brothers, Simon who was called Peter, and Andrew his brother, casting a net into the sea, for they were fishermen. And He said to them, 'Follow Me and I will make you fishers of men!' Immediately they left their nets and followed Him.*''

I definitely heard Jesus calling me. I had been chosen from before I was born. Hadn't I come into this world as the Angelus Bells were ringing? My parents were backing me all the way. I was praised for going to Mass on a Saturday morning and if I went back again for the devotions in the evening my daddy would put on my feed of bacon, eggs and black pudding before he fried some for himself, Mammy, Oliver and my new baby brother Desmond. I would be allowed to wear my Sunday clothes too. Off I'd go carrying my hat to join the crowds who were heading for The Fathers' Church.

★ ★ ★

Mammy hated our dark, cold house so Daddy set about building us a two-storey house over the bridge, off the Ennis Road, in Shelbourne Estate. The Dante brothers had become well known as building contractors in

Limerick and in six months we moved from Ryans' Cottages to Ascot House in O'Connell Avenue to Number 6 The Crescent and eventually to 49 Shelbourne Estate. But Mammy still wasn't happy. Everybody had tried to cheer her up but it was no use. She didn't love anyone even though everyone told her that they loved her.

There were times though when we did manage to enjoy ourselves. Mam and Dad got on their bicycles and cycled the three of us out into the country to collect blackberries. Sometimes we even bussed the sixty miles to Kilkee by the sea for days out and once we stayed for a whole week.

Dad and his brothers reared and trained greyhounds too and we went across the fields with Mam and Dad to practise setting them off running after a rabbit. Mam had a lovely singing voice and she enjoyed singing songs like 'This Is My Lovely Day'. However, she still cried and did strange things like cutting people out of photographs and asking why people were always reminding her of the mistakes she had made.

When we moved over the bridge to our new house in Shelbourne Estate off the Ennis Road we had to find new schools. My Granny and Granddad Colivet drove Mammy, my brother and me to the Salesian Sisters Convent School.

The nuns seemed to be young and happy. They said that their order had been started by an Italian priest in Turin, Saint John Bosco, who, less than a hundred years earlier, had followed his dream and founded an order that would concentrate on working with young people, particularly in the cities. Saint Mother Mary Mazzarello was his co-foundress. She established the Salesian Sisters whose proper title is 'Daughters of Mary Help of Christians'. John Bosco also set up a society of 'Cooperators' (lay people of any age who work alongside the priests and nuns and have their own Rule). The nuns told us they were called Salesians because John Bosco originally called them the Society of Saint Francis de Sales. Their motto was: *'Give me souls and take away everything else.'* So they, like the priests in The Fathers' Church, wanted to save the world from sin and spread the Gospel. They told us that they also did missionary work and had houses and convents as far away as Tierra del Fuego in South America.

All of us seemed attracted to these warm, welcoming and lively nuns who taught and joined in our fun and games. I fell in love with them and I enjoyed going to school so much that I also joined their 'Oratory' with its games and prayers every first Sunday of the month.

The Italian connection attracted me to them too because, on one of my visits back over the bridge to The Fathers' Church, the priest told me that I had an Italian surname. 'Imagine having the same name as the great Dante Alighieri! It was his first name but nevertheless most people just referred to him as 'Dante'. It was he who wrote the *Inferno, Purgatorio, Paradiso* and other great works.'

My family are only now, in recent years, beginning to research the origins of the name 'Dante' — and 'Colivet' too which is, of course, French — but, at that time, my apparent link to the great Dante Alighieri further convinced me that my future lay with these Irish nuns who were founded by an Italian priest who wanted to save the world.

3

Leaving Éire

All the time Mammy was saying: 'We'd be better off in England.' So in April 1955 we sold our house and furniture, said goodbye to Limerick and travelled on a train, boat, another train and a taxi to the house where my uncle had paid £5 down to reserve a flat for us. Mammy was thirty-one and pregnant with Pat, Daddy was ten years older, Des would be five that month, Oliver was eight, I was ten.

Mammy kept her eye on the meter of the taxi and when it eventually stopped outside the Shepherd's Bush address she climbed the steep steps and knocked on the door while we waited on the footpath. A scary-looking woman peered out.

I remember the thoughts that went through my head to this day.

Is she mad? Why doesn't she open the door properly? What's the chain for? Her hair's like barbed wire! Her eyes, they stick out — they're bloodshot!

'Clear off!' She was waving her fists and talking funny.

Oliver — or Tim as I had better begin calling him — was pulling Dad's pants. Des started crying.

'Where's the five pounds I sent on?' Mammy was shouting.

'Clear — off!'

No one's going to shout at my mammy! I'm going up to her!

Daddy grabbed Des and carried him up the steep steps.

'Don't move, Marion!' he shouted back. 'Tim! Sit on the cases!'

But Tim didn't.

What if he runs out on the road? He'll be killed! There's cars everywhere!

BANG! That was the door!

'Come away, Patsy!' Daddy put his arm round Mammy and led her down.

'What'll we do, Frank?'

'Well, whatever it is, we'll need food in us first. There's a place over there.'

Granny and Granddad said London's nice. Does the Queen know about this woman?

After Uncle Louis paying the five pounds you'd think she'd have to let us in. But then I don't want to live with a madwoman.

Dad took hold of the cases and Mammy grabbed the boys by the hand.

They're making to cross the road. We'll all be killed! Mam says this place is called

Shepherd's Bush. There's neither sheep nor bush, though!

Because of the cases we had to sit by the door.

'We'll have tea and ham sandwiches, please.'

'How many sandwiches, sir?'

'Butter a loaf of bread and make the tea strong.'

The man was cocking his ear at Daddy. Desmond looked funny sitting in a big chair. He'd be five in two days' time. Tim was nodding off in Dad's arms. Mammy had got that worried face on.

I was jaded. It was as though there was a film at the back of my eyes showing the entire journey from when Uncle Willie took us by car to Limerick Station and everybody was crying and waving us off. I could see us on the train. When we got off Daddy had to pull the big cases and Mammy carried Desmond, telling me to take hold of Tim's hand. (He didn't like that, now that he was eight.)

Then we were getting on the boat and trying to stay together.

Daddy found a place and it was night-time and every time I said the boat was going 'up'n down' Mammy said, 'Whist, will you?'

All night there were strange noises and

Daddy was telling Mammy to try and sleep.

They don't think I know that she's going to have another baby, but why else is she getting so fat?

The London train station was big, noisy and dark. There was lots of smoke and we didn't know a single person. In the taxi Daddy gave the man a paper with the address of the flat that Uncle Louis found for us. We didn't talk to the taxi man because we couldn't make out what he was saying!

I woke up in the restaurant now. I must have fallen asleep, snuggled up to Daddy.

'You all right, little fairy?' Daddy was patting my head.

I looked around the restaurant. The two boys were running around and the restaurant man was looking cross.

'Take her with you and I'll mind the boys,' said Daddy. 'Don't forget now, the telephone boxes'll be red.'

Mammy held out her hand. I was to go with her.

In the telephone box Mum gave me the money. It didn't have cows and horses on it but it was still silver and the same size. Even though the door was closed we could hear the traffic thudding past. Mammy was reading out the numbers, putting her finger into the hole and pushing it round. She took the money from my hand, put it in and waited.

'That you, Joyce? It's Patsy. Yes . . . we're in Shepherds' Bush. It's bad. The bitch of a woman wouldn't even let us into the place. What'll we do?' Mammy listened for a while. 'Gosh! So Brixton's far? I'd . . . Go to the police! But . . . all right . . . '

Mammy was looking at me, shaking her head. Was she going to cry? She put the phone back, took her hankie out and wiped her eyes.

'What's the police?'

'It's the 'Guards'. That's what they call them over here.'

'Are we in trouble, Mammy?'

'God, no! Aunty Joyce says Brixton's too far and it's best to get help from the Guards — the police.'

We were back. Mammy was whispering in Daddy's ear. I could hear her saying, 'I always suspected she doesn't really want us there. Should have waited 'til Brendan was home from work.' Uncle Brendan was her brother.

'They mightn't have a big enough place, Patsy. You'd never know. Maybe she's right. If we go to the Guards they'll know where we can stay for tonight and then we'll look round tomorrow.'

I was bursting to go to the toilet but didn't say anything.

Then Mammy asked, 'Where's the toilets, Frank?'

'Right in front of you.' He was pointing to a stairway with a big grey arch that went under the road. 'I'm after taking Desmond down.'

Mammy was running off, holding a hankie to her mouth, and I followed her. She was bending over and being sick in the gutter. *Yuck!*

⋆ ⋆ ⋆

Daddy was asking the restaurant man where we'd find a policeman. He was saying something but Daddy couldn't make it out. Daddy was asking again and the man opened his eyes wide and pointed. Sure enough, there was a man in blue with a helmet going past and Daddy ran out to catch him.

I didn't know what was said but soon we were in another taxi.

'Tell'em we've got money,' Mammy was telling Daddy. 'All we want is a roof over our heads tonight.'

'Didn't Joyce say we'd only eventually get a place if we say we're homeless? You saw that woman today. What if they're all like that? Louis said there's those signs, 'No Blacks. No Dogs. No Irish.''

'What'll we do, Frank?'

'Patsy, it was *you* who wanted to come over. The priests warned you.'

'That's not fair, Frank! Don't put the blame on me.'

Daddy saw me looking. He put his arm round Mammy saying, 'Sorry, Patsy.'

I hoped they wouldn't fight again.

The building we were in was big, dirty and smelly. There was another family opposite us nearly sitting on top of each other. I was hungry. The boys were falling asleep. There was hardly any light. The bulb hanging from the ceiling might go out any minute.

A woman with a greyhound's face opened a door and shouted, 'Mr and Mrs J Buckley!' in a screeching voice.

'I need to go!' Des was squealing.

The family across from us were making for the Housing woman's door. Daddy was trying to catch her before she disappeared inside again but he was too late. Mrs Buckley smiled at Daddy and pointed to a door further down. Daddy nodded, lifting Des up in his arms.

Ages seemed to go past and I was dying for my bed.

Then the door was opening again and the Housing woman was shouting, 'Mr and Mrs Dante!'

That's us.

There were only two chairs. A big old desk was separating us from the Housing woman. There were forms, brown folders and papers everywhere. The shelves behind her were stacked with folders, with the names on them facing out. The ashtray next to her was full. The air was stinking.

'You're lucky you got in. We're about to close. All I can do is take you off the road and give you a bed. By rights forms should be filled in but I understand your wife's pregnant and for that reason *only* I'll allow you to stay.'

''Tis very good of you. Patsy, my wife, can't last out and the children are starving,' answered Daddy.

'Oh, this isn't a hotel, sir! Tea and biscuits is all you'll be given here.'

She was ringing a bell. Another woman appeared at the door and was hooking her finger at us like you would to a dog. We had to follow her. She pointed to a long wooden table halfway down a smelly hall. The two lights had no shades. The floor was planky.

She was saying, 'There's tea left in the pot. There's a couple of biscuits. I'll be back to collect ye. We've space in the men's side and two beds in the women's quarters. I suggest Mr Dante keeps any valuables with him. We take no responsibility for anything that goes missing.'

Mammy started to cry. We all did, even Daddy.

'Frank, what's to become of us?'

I wonder if the Queen knows about this place.

★ ★ ★

We moved temporarily from the Rest Centre in Shepherd's Bush to our Uncle Brendan's home off Acre Lane, on the border between Brixton and Clapham. The boys got German measles and were hospitalised on account of Mammy being heavily pregnant. But even in that condition Mammy and I looked at the adverts in shop windows to try and find a flat of our own. We walked the streets and knocked on doors but once Mammy mentioned that there were three children the flat owners did not want us.

'This one wants to charge us five pounds a week for a furnished flat. That's too dear but I'm too tired and we're getting nowhere so let's knock. Holy Mother of God, please plead our case! Please, Jesus, hear your mother's prayer!' Then she whispered, 'I'll hold myself in so she won't suspect about the baby. Let you say nothing, do you hear?'

A woman with soft eyes and curly hair opened the door and smiled at me. Mammy talked and she answered in a foreign accent. She told us that she was French and married to an Englishman and that she had a daughter my age. Her name was Mrs Simmons. She showed us the kitchen, toilet and two bedrooms. Mammy accepted and paid the money and Mrs Simmons led the way upstairs and to the kitchen and then up another few steps to a double bedroom and a front room and at the top of the house to a smaller bedroom. The toilet was under the stairs opposite the door where we came in.

Soon after that my brothers were discharged from hospital and the three of us shared the bedroom at the top of the house in which there were two beds. There was no bathroom so we washed in a basin in the kitchen sink or took a towel and soap to the local baths in Clapham North. Our clothes had to be hauled to the laundrette in Acre Lane.

4

Vocation

By refusing point blank to send us to Protestant schools and badgering the headmistress, Sister Agatha, eventually Mammy managed to get us into the St Mary's Catholic School in Clapham Common.

Then in September 1956 I moved to the Holy Family Convent School in Tooting Broadway. I was eligible for a free pass as I was now travelling over three miles on two buses to get there.

There, when I was fourteen, a significant event took place which affected my whole life.

I couldn't believe my ears when Sister Sarah, a student teacher taking our class for a singing lesson, finished off the afternoon prayers with 'Mary Help of Christians, pray for us!' I recognised that prayer. Then I realised her novice's habit was familiar too.

When all the rest were leaving the class I asked Sister Sarah: 'Excuse me, Sister? You're a Salesian, aren't you?'

When she nodded smilingly I asked: 'Do you know the Sisters who run the Salesian

Convent School in Limerick?'

I took what happened next as yet another sign from God that I was to become a Salesian nun. Sister Sarah asked me if I would like to go to the Friar Park Salesian Convent in Henley-on-Thames in two weeks' time for a 'Vocations Weekend'. I was delighted and wondered if God was sending his messengers after me so that I could go and save souls. I longed for that.

I also longed for a bedroom of my own instead of having to share it with my two brothers.

* * *

'Mam, you know how you always said that I'll be a nun one day — well, some of the same nuns that taught me in Limerick are teaching for a while in our school and one of them has invited me to find out more about the life those nuns live. Can I go to a Vocations Day in Henley — not next Saturday but the next?'

* * *

I travelled on my own from Clapham Junction to attend the Vocation Day in Friar Park Convent in Henley-on-Thames. There were two other girls who stayed on that train all the way. The one who wore a brown uniform had flaxen hair swinging under a velour hat and kept looking over at me — she looked about sixteen years old. The other girl looked much older and had a missal that she was reading for most of the journey. We found the convent together.

'It's like a castle, isn't it?' said Mary, the girl with the flaxen hair.

'It's just so big and yes — like a castle! They say there are a hundred and twenty rooms in it!' said the other girl, Kathleen.

'You'd half-expect to meet a beautiful princess in bright silks and satin being driven in a glittery coach down this long tree-lined drive, wouldn't you?' I said.

'Now you're getting carried away with your fairy tales — what's your name — it's Marion, is it?' said Mary.

'To be honest, you can't blame her,' said Kathleen, 'what with the turrets and that enormous carved wooden door and just look over there to those — would you call them Italian gardens? I wouldn't be surprised to see royalty peeping through one of those oblong windows with arched tops. They say this Friar Park was built by a very rich Jew who designed it as a mixture of castle-cum-monastery.'

In later years I learned that this Victorian neo-Gothic mansion was built by the eccentric Sir Frank Crisp immortalised in the George Harrison song 'The Ballad of Sir Frankie Crisp'. George bought the house when the nuns left in 1970 and set up a recording studio there. He wrote a song about it called 'Crackerbox Palace'. Garden gnomes had been introduced while the nuns lived there and George was photographed among these for the cover of his album *All Things Must Pass* — another photo with his father and the gnomes appears on the sleeve of *Thirty Three & 1/3*.

Another interesting and ironic fact is that apparently the décor mocks organised religion — for instance, among the statues is a monk holding a skillet, with a plaque reading *'Two Holy Friars'*! I only vaguely remember this monk but I do remember that the light switches in the main building had monks' heads so you switched the lights on and off by their noses!

But George Harrison and his recording studio were all in the future the day I first arrived there.

At the door we were welcomed by a smiling nun in a full habit and a younger nun who had some of her hair showing and was without the white bonnet and bib.

My eyes were wandering all over the place trying to take in the banners and posters and literature spread out on tables, the wooden walls and pillars with ornate carvings, the big wide wooden staircase leading up to a balcony that surrounded an enormous hall on three sides.

Each of us was handed a programme in which we were informed that during this Vocation Day we would be helped to decide if God was calling us to the religious life.

There was a talk given by Mother Provincial followed by a break. Then there was a slide show on how and where the Salesian Sisters worked, explaining how they dedicated their lives to God through working with young people. After lunch, a walk round the grounds and some short prayers in chapel, the Sisters put on a film on the life of their Italian founder Saint John Bosco — or Don Bosco as he is called, 'Don' being an Italian title of respect given to priests.

The culmination of the day of course was the celebration of the Holy Mass. I loved all the cheerful singing, and the warm feeling I sensed right inside myself told me that God was pleased with me.

★ ★ ★

'Well, are you going to join up?' asked another girl, Virginia, on our way home on the train.

'Yes. I can't wait to get my mother to fill in these forms. How about you?'

'Now, I don't want to put you off and I think you're great for giving everything up, but I want to get married and have children. I love kids.'

All I could think of was Mammy crying all the time and waiting for Daddy to come home and the three of us kids being squashed into a small bedroom and not being allowed to touch anything because it wasn't our furniture and being forbidden to go out and have fun like we did back in Ireland. I hated it all and certainly did not want to have a breakdown like my mam because she never seemed to get over it, even though she prayed. She was mostly sick and miserable and always wanted to be somewhere else.

'Well, my mother always tells me and everybody else that she's so proud of me because I'm going to be a nun,' I said. 'It's like that's all that matters to her. It makes her feel so happy and she says that God is pleased with her when she offers me to Him.'

'But what do *you* want? Would you prefer to get married and have children?'

'And be unhappy like my mother? No, I

can't wait to get away from home.'

When I got home my parents were in bed but I went straight in to their room. 'I want to be a nun — a Salesian nun. Would you let me?'

Mammy looked delighted and said: 'If that's what you really want we won't stand in your way, will we, Frank?'

Dad said nothing, then he laughed and turned over.

Mum poked him, asking: 'Frank, what d'you think?'

'Ah, sure there's no hurry. Go to bed now and we'll talk some other time.'

I prayed: *Jesus, I'm special. I'm chosen. You are really calling me. I was looking for the Salesian Convent in Chertsey that the nuns in Limerick told me about but I couldn't find it — well, I had the name wrong — I thought it was called 'Churchsey'. And what do you do but send these nuns to my school and to top it all they're looking for people to join up! What more proof do I need?*

At my Tooting Broadway convent school things were just beginning to get a bit awkward and embarrassing because during the lunch hour my friends had begun to discuss embarrassing things. Nearly all of us thought Cliff Richard and Elvis Presley were great but some girls wanted to talk about kissing and going out with boys. I loved going dancing and looking at the pictures of these stars but I could feel flushes and a strange mixture of feeling wet and weak and excited and happy all at the same time and I wondered if God was pleased with this.

'Come on, let's walk around the garden with Sister Mary of the Sacred Heart! She's only got two girls with her today. Come on, Valerie!'

The nun on duty used to walk round the garden to keep an eye on everyone and those of us who chose to do so — a select group — would accompany her, walking backwards so as to face her. A couple of girls could walk on either side of her too but the path round the garden was not very wide and so the rest followed this strange custom of facing her out of respect.

I felt good and holy and different walking backwards and facing Sister Mary of the Sacred Heart in her long black swishing habit, and besides I knew she thought highly of me after I told her that I was going to start my training to be a nun that August.

One day when Sister Mary asked me if I was too hot wearing my navy blazer I told her that I'd grown out of my cardigan and, as I had been told to be modest and cover up my body, I would have to wear my blazer even though it was a hot summer. I didn't tell her though that on the Vocation Day the Salesian Sisters' novice mistress had also recommended that I needed to brush my teeth better!

My friend Margaret Reilly tried to put me off entering a convent by saying that nuns say a lot of prayers, but I was used to prayers, what with going to the Novena in Limerick and so on. Also, we had always prayed the Rosary at home. We'd kneel on the seats of chairs and recite the five decades and then add on prayers for all our intentions. Of course, once it had been agreed that I was going away to be a nun that was mentioned in these prayers.

Besides, it wouldn't all be prayer — this order of nuns was more active and into teaching and looking after young people.

I really achieved notoriety when the school year was closing and it was announced at assembly that although I was only in third year I was leaving the school in July to enter a convent and start my training as a nun.

5

Leaving Home

I was fourteen years old and was to enter the convent at Sandgates, Chertsey on 24th August 1959. I'd been given a list of things I had to take with me and I'd got the interlock vests and knickers, and the thick lisle stockings, and had even ordered the 'Cash's names' to be stitched on to label my clothes. ('Cash's names' were embroidered names that were stitched onto all school clothes. You went to a store with your own name printed clearly and selected the type of print and colour that you wanted. This instruction was sent off and after a week you collected bundles of small pieces of material with your name stitched on them. No doubt 'Cash' was the trade name.)

All that was left was the shoes.

According to the list I was supposed to have black lace-ups, but right in front of me in the window of Dolcis Shoe Shop was a pair of red slip-ons that I had been eyeing all week. I just *loved* them. They had three little buttons on top that were like smiling faces with twinkling eyes. What was I to do? I decided there would be no harm in trying them on.

They're pure lovely and I look grown up in them and I am nearly fifteen. They're so shiny and red and Mam's given me the money. My case is nearly packed, so I can easily hide them underneath something. The shop assistant's waiting. I'll walk around and look in the mirror again.

My feet were hot and sticky with excitement and the woman was asking, 'Well?'

I bought the red Dolcis slip-ons and ran all the way home, planning what I was going to say, but my mam was so busy cooking Sunday dinner on Thursday in honour of my leaving home that she didn't question me. I hid the shoes in the suitcase inside the dressing-gown she had given me.

Dad was very quiet. He kept looking at something far away, then when our eyes met he'd put his head down.

When I left he didn't kiss me goodbye. I wondered about that. Perhaps he thought that I wouldn't last out in the convent or I'd just change my mind and come home.

It was hard to know what to do for the best. The previous weekend I'd slept at Aunty Joyce and Uncle Brendan's house. She was

very good-looking and wore her hair in a
French roll and he was like Robert Mitchum.
I spent a long time in their bath making
lovely smelly bubbles. They'd got any amount
of hot water. I suppose I soaked for ages on
account of us not having a bath of our own
and being forced to walk all the way down to
Lambeth Public Baths. Anyway my aunt and
uncle seemed to be waiting for me when I
came out. They sat me down and asked me
lots of questions. It was as though they were
trying to persuade me that joining the
convent was a bad idea. Imagine! How could
I ignore the call of all those poor souls in
Africa? Aunty Joyce was not a Catholic so she
had never heard the priests saying: 'Many are
called, but few are chosen.'

It was nice being chosen and special but I
liked jiving with Margaret and Valerie too.
We'd all had a terrific time the previous
Saturday when a group of us went to Tooting
Bec Parish disco. There were boys there and I
was swung round by one of them. I got all hot
and excited. I was wearing my cotton half-slip
with a yard and a half of washing-line run
through the hem of it, so it stuck right out.
Valerie was turned right over by another
fellow and you could see her knickers!

Mam didn't know about the three of us
getting off the bus the other day on the way

home from school to see *Jailhouse Rock*. That Elvis Presley was something else! We were in our posh navy-blue school uniforms: velour hats, gloves, blazers with braiding, shining school badges, the lot! So when the usherette shone her light along our row, she never suspected it was us shouting out and singing loudly.

I felt great and 'groovy' and I wanted to wear my flared skirt and dance and dance.

But that was last week. I'd given up all that hilarity and I was on my way to the convent now. I hated saying goodbye to Mam, my two brothers and baby sister at Clapham Junction. No one cried. Mam was too busy giving me half a crown to get a taxi from Chertsey Station to the convent and the boys were excited. I expect they liked seeing the trains. What with the pram and my case and opening and shutting the door, the train was moving off before I felt tears trickling down my cheeks.

I could still go back. But then I was fed up sharing a room with my brothers and it wasn't our house and we were always having to be quiet. Why did we ever leave the lovely home Dad had built in Ireland?

'If We Only Had Old Ireland Over Here!'

Isn't that a grand song? Wouldn't it be great if we had the green fields and the seaside at Kilkee over here?

But at least these nuns I was going to join were the same kind that taught me in Limerick and once I was trained, I'd be off saving all those black babies out in darkest, pagan Africa.

★　★　★

The taxi man had driven me up the long tree-lined lane, handed me my case, taken the fare and left me in the porch. The doors were so big and there was a grille over the side window.

They're taking a long time answering the bell! Perhaps they're in chapel. Oh, now I can hear the big key turning.

'You're welcome! It's Marion, Marion Dante, isn't it? You're the last to arrive. Remember me? I'm Sister Hilda. Come in. The Sisters will be out of chapel soon. Supper's at six so you'll have time to unpack and dress in something more suitable.'

No hugs or handshaking. This puckered-faced nun lifted wrinkly hands to adjust her black veil while looking me up and down.

Does she think my lovely green skirt, white blouse and navy jacket are not up to the mark? Is that why she's in such a hurry for me to change? I expect she prefers us all to be in black. What would she say if she laid eyes on my red slip-ons?

Then she put on a saintly smile and signalled me in to a large entrance hall with a high ceiling, a polished parquet floor and a huge picture of Our Lady and Baby Jesus over a mantelpiece. When I looked over my right shoulder I noticed a statue of Mary Immaculate on the window ledge halfway up the wide stairs. There was another flight beyond that going up even further.

'Come along now,' she said and I wondered which of the five dark wooden doors with brass handles she was going to take me through. First she checked that the front door behind me was locked and I wanted to run back out. But I didn't.

Sister Hilda led me through the door to my left. The floor was hard and stony. There were black and dark-blue garments neatly hanging from coat-pegs high up on the wall on my right and we passed the grille-windowed washroom on the left. Again to the left we climbed wooden stairs that were narrow, winding and echoey. She crept and shuffled in worn-down black lace-ups and it was eerily quiet. The dormitory was in the attic and there were white curtains around beds with white candlewick bedspreads. She told me rules about what you couldn't have in your locker and about how you had to wash in a basin on a stand at the foot of your bed. There was a jug to be filled with water. There was any amount of regulations concerning silence. I was allowed to put my nightclothes under my pillow, so I decided that's where I'd hide my Dolcis shoes.

I'd no sooner started to unpack than a massive clanger of a bell belted out and Sister Hilda began the Angelus. Coming from Ireland, I knew fine well that this prayer was recited three times a day to remind us all that when God sent the Angel Gabriel to ask Mary if she'd be God's Mother she said yes. Didn't my own mother tell me that I was born when the Angelus Bell was ringing back in the Franciscan Church in Limerick and wasn't that partly why I was here today imitating Mary's generosity in offering my life to God for the service of others?

It was years later I was to discover that, because I was conceived out of wedlock, my mother had decided then that I would be her 'sin offering'.

★ ★ ★

I'd been here three days. There were twenty-four aspirants — that's twenty-four females wanting to be nuns. Some were really old, as ancient as thirty, and others were even younger than me and I was only fourteen. Two were just starting secondary school so that made them eleven. The oldest woman came from Italy and the three from Malta looked fairly old too. So did the two Dutch girls. Two others were like me because they lived in England but were really Irish. Then there was lovely Monique who was French of course and the five from Scotland who had made it quite clear that they were not English or even British. And they were 'Scots' not 'Scottish'. They said they were 'Father Daly's vocations', which meant that he'd recruited them. When school started one of them turned out to be my PE teacher.

Clothes had been distributed to all of us the day we arrived. Those of us who were of school uniform age were each given a hand-me-down navy and white school uniform and, for Sundays and feast days, a black serge uniform dress. The dress had a detachable white starched collar and six small white pearl buttons down the middle of the bodice, with two on each cuff of the long sleeves. We had brought our underwear and brown lisle stockings from home. Later, in winter, we would be glad of the woollen vests we had brought because the furnace to heat the pipes was rarely on.

I didn't know how to hide my shoes at night. Then I decided to slide one shoe down between my sheets either side of the mattress — both top and bottom sheets were always firmly tucked under the mattress on each side. When Sister Hilda passed by our row of beds I was petrified to move in case a shoe fell out on the floor. I felt guilty for hiding my red slip-ons, but if I handed them in I might never get them back. I could even be sent home. Then again I wasn't sure about staying here forever. We were having to work all day and then there were the prayers — the Rosary, Mass, Benediction, morning and night prayers and many more. We even had to recite a psalm in Latin called 'The *Miserere*' when we were getting ready for bed.

At six in the morning a nun rang a bell and called out '*Benedicamus Domino!*' (Let us bless the Lord!) In perfect silence, we had to make our beds, wash in our basins, dress, take turns in the toilets, creep downstairs, put our veils on, and line up outside chapel to be led in to the front benches so that we could join the nuns for prayers and Mass.

There are so many rules! Sometimes I'd just like to make a run for it through the rhododendron bushes and hide and read a book, or just go for a walk into the woods on my own. But the nuns keep reminding us that

50

the devil finds work for idle hands. Besides, there are signs up everywhere saying 'God sees me'.

★ ★ ★

Margaret P was good fun. There was a glint in her eye. Today nearly all the aspirants had been told to clean the school. The two of us had been given the job of washing out the girls' toilets. We were out of earshot of everyone else so I started singing Cliff Richard's 'Living Doll'. We ended up jiving. I told her about my slip-on shoes and she said she'd got proper Scottish dancing pumps with her.

'I'll go mad, Margaret, if I don't dance!'

'So will I, Marion! So how about we get our dancing shoes and let rip?'

At that moment Sister Hilda popped her head round the door, looked as though she could see into our souls and then went away.

Has she heard us? Will she report us? Is God cross?

★ ★ ★

When the lights went off in the dormitory that night I couldn't sleep. I heard Sister Hilda, who as the nun responsible for the aspirants slept with us in the dormitory, pulling the curtains round her bed, tiptoeing out to the washroom, coming back and getting into bed. It was darker now and there was snoring and someone was talking in her sleep. What was that? Monique next to me had a fit of coughing. Now someone was brushing right against my bed.

Oh my God, there goes a shoe! Phew! I've rescued it. Thank God it's dark. That was close!

I can't go on like this. It's no use. I feel so guilty. All those times set apart for examining my conscience make me think I've sinned. I'll have to tell the priest when I go to confession. Jesus won't be pleased with me because I'm not honest and upright. Besides, you're not really supposed to have secrets. I'll just have to wear my red slip-ons! I'll put them on for country dancing tomorrow night.

We'd been sent to the dormitory to change. I went up last, so there would be no one else around. Even so I pulled my curtains before taking my red slip-ons out from under my pillow. What was I to do? It was like their smiling button faces were appealing for mercy. I loved these shiny red shoes. I smelt the soft rosy leather and pressed them to my cheeks and kissed them one at a time. I put on white socks and slipped on my gorgeous red shoes. As if by magic my feet began to tap and before I knew it I was dancing and remembering the fun times I had jiving with Valerie and Margaret and my friends. *What's that noise? Oh God, someone else must have come up to get changed. I'd better to join the others.*

I pulled myself together and went down.

'Marion, are those dancing shoes you are wearing?'

'They are light and easy to move about in, Sister Hilda.'

'When you've finished that dance I'd like to have a word with you.'

'Certainly, Sister Hilda.'

I'm in for it now! Sister Hilda looks fierce as the big black raven with clipped wings that I've seen in the Tower of London.

'Marion Dante, red slip-on shoes are too worldly for aspirants. I'll give you a bottle of black dye tonight.'

Sister Hilda smiled benignly and I felt sick.

6

Aspirant

'*Benvenuta, Madre!* Blow your snooter, Madre!'

After weeks of yanking up massive big brambles, weeding, felling trees, cutting wood, mowing grass, hauling furniture about, we awaited the arrival of the Mother General of The Daughters of Mary Help of Christians (otherwise known as the Salesian Sisters) from Turin, Italy. One minute we would be filthy dirty, thirsty and sweating in the summer heat and the next we would find ourselves learning how to sing hymns and songs in preparation.

My friend Maeve Roach and I were told to clear the neglected 'Path of Perfection' leading away from the convent to the new Saint John Bosco's Grammar School. The Path of Perfection had plants on either side that had to be constantly weeded and raked. I presume it was given that name to remind us that we had begun to live a life that would eventually lead to Perfection. Neither of us knew one end of a hoe from the other and there we were hacking weeds and pulling out big prickly brambles. We worked for hours on end knowing that there would be no let up.

By the time Mother General arrived in September we had learnt how to survive on a meagre diet and sleep from pure exhaustion. Any clothes we had brought from home were well worn and those of us who were still of school age looked forward to having a uniform. Unfortunately we soon discovered that this would also be second-hand, well worn and often patched.

The enormous red-bricked mansion we scrubbed, rubbed and tried to keep clean was dilapidated, inadequately heated and sadly lacking in facilities. Beyond the polished wooden façade, where we lived in the servants' quarters, cold concrete, floorboards and faded paintwork were a constant reminder that we had opted to live for the next life in heaven.

'*Benvenuta, Madre!* Blow your snooter, Madre!'

'Shsh! They'll hear you!'

The nuns were too overawed to suspect that we, whom they referred to as 'the future of the congregation' would ever make fun of their Italian welcome. But how else were we teenagers to cope with work followed by prayers and prayers followed by work?

However, I continued to believe that I had been chosen by God and I certainly was not going home to a furnished flat and a needy family. So I resorted to being a clown and was often told off for either causing others to laugh or laughing too heartily. The number of times Sister Aileen, our assistant in the *aspirantade*, told me not to throw my head back, open my mouth wide and laugh so raucously!

I performed a solo piece that was often requested and considered to be really funny — I suppose because it made a skit of the fact that, as most of us didn't speak the Queen's English, we were given elocution lessons.

I'd begin reciting this poem in my cultured elocution voice:

'*The swallow is a roving bird. Each year he flies to Spain*

(I'd accompany this with appropriate actions of course)

And when the summer comes once more he flies back home again!

(At this point I'd adopt a husky Cockney accent)

But on the 'omeward journey he met a flipping 'awk

What whipped off all his feathers and said now you'll have to walk!'

And so on.

Three of us — Maeve, Mandy and I — eventually formed a performing group. We did what we called 'sketches'. It was like acting out a joke and timing the punch line. Whenever there was a feast-day (a saint's day or other religious festival) or a visitor was to be entertained, like Mother Provincial or a missionary Sister, we'd be asked to get a performance ready. Sometimes, in fact most times, we'd do more laughing while we were preparing than anyone would at the performance.

A favourite sketch involved dressing up in fire-brigade helmets we'd acquired from the Infants' dressing-up box. We'd each carry a bucket and have a ladder between us. Then we'd rush on, looking as though we'd arrived at the scene of a fire. We'd put the ladder down and in chorus, while we raised our arms and contorted our faces into pained expressions, in plaintive Cockney accents we'd say:

'And the flames went up and up and there framed in the first-storey window was a human face and a voice what screamed 'Save me, save me!'

And we said, 'ere (pointing down) jump onto this tarpaulin what me and my mates has brought. But she wouldn't!'

Then we'd repeat this saying 'the second

storey' and the next time 'the third storey'!

Then came the punch line: *'Then she jumped! But we had forgotten the tarpaulin!'*

In fact, apart from the fun we made ourselves, we had almost no entertainment. On a big occasion, when the television was rolled in, it was covered with a shawl so that once it was switched on we would not be able to view anything before the Sister in charge had a look under the shawl and assured herself that it was suitable for us. To make matters worse, the nuns were not accustomed to using TVs so there was always a great deal of trying to find out how to operate it and we had to wait for ages, staring at this shawl, before the show was on the road.

Even when Princess Margaret was getting married and the Sisters and aspirants were all seated in the refectory facing the TV, full of anticipation, one of the Sisters took off the black shawl she had round her shoulders and draped it over the television. Then she made sure that the volume was turned down so that we could neither see nor hear anything while she checked it out! That became very amusing because the shawl kept slipping and sliding off the television set, causing us to snigger and laugh.

We had left the world outside of the convent walls so everything — our post, what we said to our parents and family members, our very thoughts — had to be purified so that we could become more and more like the saints. Our Lady and Our Lord were the highest models that we were aspiring to imitate.

We never saw a newspaper and when it was considered that something of significance was happening in the world outside the headmistress nun would pin bits of newspaper articles that she had cut out on a notice board.

Our incoming and outgoing post was censored. On the first Sunday of the month we sat in the study and were supervised as in silence we wrote our letters home. These would be handed in and checked for content, spelling, punctuation and presentation and then be posted by one of the Sisters. Although I often begrudged the fact that I could not express my real feelings, sometimes I was glad the nuns read my letters — for instance, I enjoyed the fact that they came to know that my family was moving house yet again.

Those of us who were still of school age found it very difficult to study as I expect the teachers among us experienced difficulties preparing their lessons. We started with prayers in chapel and Mass from six thirty to seven thirty. Then we each had a 'charge', or a part of the house which was assigned to us to sweep and dust each day. A bell would go at five to eight and we had to be standing behind our chairs in the refectory when the second bell rang and 'Grace Before Meals' was started by the Sister in charge. We were allowed to speak while we ate bread that had already been given just a scrape of butter. Two of us took turns in collecting a big tinny teapot put through the hatch by the Sister in the kitchen. Tea that was already milked, sugared and often stewed was poured into cups in a row at the bottom of each table. These were passed up the table to each aspirant. After breakfast we either washed up, tidied and prepared the refectory for dinner, finished off our 'charge' or, if it was not our turn for these tasks, we could go to the study. At approximately eight forty those of us in school followed the Path of Perfection and then across the hockey field to be in time to join our classes at nine. We had our dinner back in the convent after morning classes. Again we took turns at either serving or washing the dishes or pots or the kitchen floor after the meal.

So the routine continued. After school when the girls went home, we cleaned the school and pushed the leftover school dinners and milk in a wooden cart to the house. We had tea, prayed the Rosary and had fifteen minutes of spiritual literature read to us in chapel. Then we studied and went for supper at seven thirty. Once more we washed and tidied up and then, weather permitting, went outside and played or learnt games in preparation for our work with young people once we were nuns.

We played the ordinary games of rounders, tennis, netball and games like 'Cat and Mouse' for the younger child. The only unusual game I can remember was a type of netball game called *'Tre Punti'* in which all twenty of us were split into two opposing teams and the object of the game was for all the players on one team to manage to cross over to the other side of the net. When someone succeeded in catching the ball three times, they could cross over and try and rescue another member of their team by throwing it to her three times.

Recreation was brought to a close by the 'goodnight'. This was a tradition that Don Bosco started. The purpose of it was that we listened to an uplifting or inspirational speech before we went to bed each night. So we stood in a semicircle, sang a hymn and listened to the superior of the aspirants or her assistant. Then in silence we followed each other into chapel for night prayers at nine, after which we went quietly to the dormitory and joined in the recitation of the *Miserere* as we prepared for bed. This strict timetabling was slightly altered at weekends when, once we had spent most of the morning cleaning, we sometimes were sent for a walk or we could be told to do some gardening. On Sunday, of course, the prayers and the Mass took longer and we played hockey after dinner and could read approved books, write home or do our homework before Benediction of The Blessed Sacrament in the evening. On feast-days there were more prayers and singing but also more food. Some of us belonged to the choir while the rest prepared the vegetables when this was going on.

We were not permitted to talk or mix with the day pupils at the school and were conspicuous by the dowdy versions of the uniform that we wore. As we donned overalls and began cleaning the school before the girls left for home each evening, they seemed to look down on us. Even the nuns who taught us became exasperated with the fact that our energy was sapped and they saw us working when we should have been studying and consequently rarely managed to give our homework in on time.

★   ★   ★

I slowly became institutionalised by the constant routine of convent life over the four years I spent as an aspirant and postulant. Then in 1963 when I moved to Friar Park and became a novice, convent life became even more rule-bound. In fact the Rule states:

'The noviciate is the period of real initiation into the religious life. Through reflection on the Word of God, diligent study and assimilation of the Constitutions, daily effort in self-discipline, and the integration of work and prayer, the novice will understand ever better the demands of following Christ . . . '

Old Father Sherlock, our resident priest, reminded us that he had taken the 'Pledge' (of total abstinence from alcohol) yet he accepted *zabaglione* laced with wine each noon before his dinner. Nevertheless he made us learn the definition of 'conscience' off by heart from our text, Harte's Christian Doctrine: *'Conscience is the eye by which we measure the light of nature.'*

Over the two years noviciate I became used to scrutinising my every motive and desire while my *Signora Maestra* (novice mistress) and her assistants analysed and assessed my suitability for this way of life.

However, we were encouraged by the fact that we now, at last, felt like proper nuns! As postulants we wore a black shop-bought skirt with a white blouse, black stockings and a black cardigan or jumper. It felt like a school uniform, the big difference being that a postulant received her cape on 31st January, the Feast of Saint John Bosco. This was made of black serge and had a little stand-up collar and was worn over the cardigan, reaching to the waist, with poppers down the front that were hidden under a strip of material. But now, as novices, we wore a habit the same as the Sisters except that we had no *modestino* (a white starched bib) and our veils had no white pieces underneath so some of our hair was visible in front. But it had to be kept well back and tamed down and no fringes were allowed.

The noviciate was tough for many reasons but most of all because we were driven by a very demanding and dominant Italian novice mistress, Sister Maria Teresa Pranzo, who had been my Sister Superior in the *aspirantade*. She found it difficult not to be partial and lacked understanding of human nature.

I recall her calling me up to the top table where she and her two assistants sat apart from us. She asked me to turn my head so that she could see my ears. When I did she said, 'Your ears are small and the best part of you but soon they will be covered with a veil forever.'

I always smile when I recall the occasion when during our second year in the noviciate we were instructed that if we withheld any information concerning our health our vows would be null and void. By that time we had all become so scrupulous and nervous that when I began to feel pains in my chest I feared I might be about to have a heart attack. So I waited behind when everyone else left the refectory after breakfast and owned up to my suspected ill health. Sister Maria Teresa and the assistant looked at each other and I was told to report back if these pains continued.

Then I noticed a smile coming over the assistant's face as she said, 'Maybe it would be a good idea to look and see if there's a button sticking into you.'

Sure enough, when I did examine my underwear I found that my bulging 'piety bag' containing a relic and medal was rubbing against my chest. Needless to say when I dutifully reported back on this, even Sister Maria Teresa allowed a glimmer of a smile to cross her severe lips.

Because I was convinced that I had been

chosen by God to help save as many souls as possible from sin and hell, I persevered despite any other doubts that troubled me. Of course returning to a troubled home was never an option for me. Besides, I rarely suffered ill health and was robust and strong and that was said to be a sign of a vocation.

7

Profession Day

So I was married to God on 5th August 1965 in the house later bought and immortalised by the Beatle George Harrison. But the Beatles were far from my mind in the run-up to that particular day.

It was the feast day of Our Lady of the Snows who had caused a miraculous shower of snow to fall on a hill where she wished a church to be built in her honour, on a hot August day in Rome in 358 A.D.

Aged twenty, I was the second youngest of seven novices who made the vows of Poverty, Chastity and Obedience in Friar Park Convent in Henley-on-Thames.

I had been an aspirant for three and a half years, a postulant for six months, and a novice for two years. In preparation for our big day, the seven of us together with Sisters from some of our other convents, took part in a retreat of eight days' reflection and prayer during which we received sermons on topics relating to the vows we were soon to make.

'Try not to get too excited tonight, novices.

Now I suppose you have heard that it has become a tradition to have a camomile drink to help you sleep tonight. So after night prayers you'll find that Sister will have a jug in the refectory for you to drink there. Remember though that you must keep the silence.'

'Yes. Thank you, *Signora Maestra!*' we chorused.

As she walked away Maeve jumped up in the air, clapping and exclaiming, '*Yippee! We've made it! Well, almost!*'

The seven of us had been walking up and down in front of the convent after our evening meal. It was recreation time. When the *Signora Maestra* had gone back into the convent we huddled round our assistant and tried to address our fears.

I asked, 'Sister Anne, did you feel collywobbles before you were professed?'

'Of course . . . what are you two whispering about? Tell us all.'

Two red-faced novices looked at each other before one of them confessed, 'Sister Anne, it's just . . . well, what I said is that it will take more than camomile tea to get me to sleep tonight!'

We all laughed and Sister Anne asked, 'You weren't expecting a strong whiskey by any chance?'

I was delighted that we had begun to air our fears because I was worried and frightened and delighted all at the same time. I had found it very hard to sleep almost every night during the retreat. Things were getting very serious and I wondered if I had made the right decision, but then all the others seemed to be behaving as though they were OK with things so why shouldn't I be?

'Look, it is natural for you to be worried about the big commitments you will be making tomorrow. Why do you think Signora Maestra came out here to tell you about a drink to calm you down? Every year novices get worked up and frightened on the eve of their big day. Pray. Talk to your future Spouse. Tell Him what is on your mind. Use one of the aspirations that were suggested in the retreat when you are trying to go to sleep: 'Jesus, I want to live and work for you! Jesus, I love you, help me to show your love to others! Let your love shine through me!''

The tea was lukewarm and little bits of the camomile leaves were still floating around in it but it did the job and once the lights were out I eventually managed to fall asleep, reciting the suggested aspirations or 'ejaculations' as they were also called! But then I woke bolt upright in the middle of the night and had to creep out to the toilet. I couldn't put the light on because I would wake the three others who shared the room. But I must have wakened the novice in the corner because she and I tossed and turned through a very long night and right up until the *'Benedicamus'*.

'Remember you have a long day in front of you. We will be in chapel for an hour or two. So be sensible, eat plenty of bread and butter even if you feel you don't need it,' announced *Signora Maestra* after we were seated for breakfast after morning prayer.

I forced myself to eat a slice and a half and two cups of tea before we were told to go up to the dormitory where we would meet the 'Guardian Angels' assigned to us who would help us get dressed in our white dresses.

'Marion, Marion!'

I heard the whisper and felt the tug and turned to see Maeve's ashen face.

'Have you been sick?' she asked. 'And my head feels like it's going to burst.'

'Stop! I feel as though I could . . . '

Just then our dressers arrived.

My dresser, Sister Angelica, was great because she was not at all surprised at me being scared of taking this big step and yet proud of having reached this big day. My feelings were very muddled. The white dress was well worn and not at all like a bridal dress. But I wanted to fulfil my dreams. I knew my mother would be very proud of me. I was about to achieve what I had set out to do. God would be pleased at me. But I was perspiring and shaking and frightened of walking down the stairs to the chapel. What if I slipped?

When the music for the 'Veni, Sponsa Christi' ('Come, Spouse of Christ') began I floated into line and was carried dreamlike into the chapel.

It was only after I had returned to the dormitory, came back down dressed in my new black habit and was actually about to say my name aloud when making my vows that I remembered that there was a congregation present and my family was there. I knew my mother would be ecstatic and I knew that my dad would love hearing his name 'Dante'. That was one thing that he liked about the Salesians: the fact that when you joined up you kept your own name. Don Bosco wanted his religious to live as closely to the lay community as possible and be 'good citizens of the world'. Accordingly, we kept our everyday names instead of being endowed with fancy religious ones. One of the advantages of this was that we had no problems when filling in legal forms whereas other Religious did. The downside was that there could be a profusion of common names like 'Mary' and 'Anne' and 'Margaret' in one community which could at times lead to confusion.

I suspected that Dad had never wanted me to be a nun but today he would be proud of me nevertheless. I was so glad I was being a credit to my family. I was also pleased that I was going to be able to save their souls too. I could do that now because we had been told that, once we were fully fledged Sisters, Don Bosco had promised that not only we would be saved, but those in our family to the third generation.

★ ★ ★

'That was so long!' My ten-year-old sister Pat heaved a massive sigh when we eventually emerged from chapel.

'It's a relief to get it over at last!' I said.

'I can imagine, what with having to keep quiet for eight whole days leading up to it!' said Mam.

'But we didn't have to keep silence all the time! Every day we were allowed to talk during recreation for almost an hour after dinner and supper and at other times too. I mean it's not as though we never heard our own voices. We said our prayers aloud and we sang hymns and went to Confession, and things like that.'

We sat next to Maeve and her parents around a long table set for eighteen and waited to be served our soup.

'I bet you didn't sleep a wink last night?' said Mam.

'I did, you know, Mam. We were drugged! No, I'm joking, of course. We were given a cup of camomile tea before bed. I was nervous though about making these vows. '

'Vows? What are they?' enquired Pat.

'Solemn promises. There are three. First, Poverty means that I own nothing and I have to work. Chastity is to do with not getting married and trying to think pure thoughts and things like that. And Obedience — well, you know what that means. I've to do as I'm told and go wherever I'm sent.'

'That'll be a change!' laughed Dad. 'No, I'm joking. You're a credit to us.'

'Don't start us off again now, Frank. We've done enough crying during the Mass and everything!' said Mam, wiping her tears away.

One of the Sisters arrived with the soup. It was so hot that it steamed up her glasses. I stood up to begin ladlling it out while she took them off and put them in her pocket.

Mrs Roach leaned over to address Mam: 'Haven't you got two boys, Mrs Dante?'

'You're right and we have another daughter Bernadette. She's too young to bring. But we were told that young men are not allowed on account of the day that's in it. Then again they didn't really want to come . . . you know how it is . . . ?'

While the soup plates were collected and the dinner served, Maeve and I were plied with questions over the ceremony.

'Were you supposed to be a bride in that white dress?' Pat wanted to know.

'Yes, the Bride of Christ,' said Mam.

'You went out in white and came back very quickly dressed in black,' said Pat. 'Was there someone helping you to change?'

'Yes, we were each given a Guardian Angel in the shape of a Sister who dressed us and kept us calm. Sister Angelica was mine.'

'Was it a proper wedding dress?' Pat wanted to know.

'No. Remember this ceremony takes place every year so a number of various sizes of plain full-length white dresses were taken out and allotted to us according to size.'

'It was so touching!' said Mam, her eyes filling up again. 'Especially when ye filed in and the priest asked, 'What is it you want?' and ye said ye wanted to become Brides of Christ!'

'I can still hear the 'Veni, Sponsa Christi',

can you, Marion?' asked Maeve and we both burst into the first few bars of it.

'That was our wedding march, Pat!' I said. 'It means 'Come, Spouse of Christ'!'

Pat was looking at my new crucifix. 'There's FMA written on one side!'

'Yes, standing for *Figlie di Maria Ausiliatrice* — Daughters of Mary Help of Christians. That's a sign that each one of us is now on the cross with Jesus.'

Mrs Roach had produced a packet of tissues and they were all stretching to grab some to swab their eyes.

'Why had some of the nuns pink crowns of roses but yours are white?' asked Pat.

'Well, we made our vows for the first time but the ones who got pink crowns of roses were renewing their vows for life.'

Once the 'Grace After Meals' was said, my mother and Mrs Roach went off to chat together and our dads went for a walk round the beautiful Friar Park grounds while my curious sister cross-examined Maeve and me about what we were wearing under those black habits.

We sat on a bench underneath a sturdy oak tree with an old towel under us to protect our new habits.

'Do you really make your own underwear or were you joking me?' asked Pat.

'Yes, and it's not easy! I had to rip out the machine stitching so often that mine became a pale shade of grey! Our knickers are made of stiff white calico — four pieces cut from a pattern, machine-stitched and held together by a waistband, two buttons and lots of coarse white tape. And they have to be long enough to cover over our knees!'

Pat's eyes were sparkling through her long blonde hair. 'I can't believe you said knickers! I bet that my shorts are shorter than those pants! What else do you wear?'

'A woolly vest in winter and an interlock one in the summer. And a black cotton half-length petticoat which again is drawn into a waistband with a button and black tape wrapped round the waist.'

'And in bed we wear a chemise!' said Maeve. 'We had to sew those too!'

'What's a chemise?'

'It's long and white and made of cotton material,' said Maeve. 'It's like a T-shirt except it reaches from the neck to below the knees with long sleeves and an opening to get your head through. And four buttons from the centre-neck down.'

'And I'll tell you something that will horrify you!' I said. 'We wear chemises in the bath too!' It didn't seem right to tell her it was to prevent us looking at our own bodies. So I

76

didn't and was thankful that she didn't ask.

'How can you wash yourself? It must have gone all soggy and clingy. *Yuk!* That's stupid!'

I wanted to tell her she was right but instead got up and started to do a mimic of the catwalk, saying: 'And now the dress! The dress is made from black serge.' I pointed. 'The bodice is lined and the edges of the sleeves are trimmed with cord and two tiny dinky buttons. The bodice is attached by hand-stitching to this ankle-length black skirt of the same material. Note it is flat at the front and gathered into tiny pleats in a bustle fashion at the back. It has a deep hem and again the bottom of the skirt is trimmed with hand-made cord.'

'Very figure-flattering!' laughed Maeve. 'It sticks out at the bottom like a crinoline.'

To Pat's applause, I continued with my catwalk and commentary: 'A straight, black cotton apron is worn over this habit, reaching to the ankle and around the sides of the wearer. This apron is pleated into a waistband and secured and tied with yet more black tape. Oh yes, notice the bib which we call the *modestino*.'

'*Modestino?* What a funny word!'

'As you can see, it is a white starched calico oval piece of material which has a stand-up collar and two buttons at the back of the neck. It reaches from the neck to three-quarters of the way down the cape. Unfortunately I have already splashed a tiny drop of soup on it so I will be glad to be wearing a plastic everyday version tomorrow instead of this stiffly starched calico one. However, I have been advised that the plastic one gets very hot and brittle from body heat and eventually becomes yellow and breaks up.' I plumped down on the bench. 'I forgot the cape! You'll have to do that, Maeve. But, Pat, don't laugh too loud. Eyes are turning this way. Just keep your voice a little lower. OK?'

Sister Maeve was soon in full flow: 'The cape as you might have guessed goes over the shoulders and again is made of black serge. It has no collar as such and reaches down to the waist, covering the arms and is joined in front with six fasteners. It is the epitome of modesty, covering all traces of bosoms and cancelling out the need of a bra!'

'Oh! I'm telling. You said bra!'

'Now for the headgear.'

'Have you still got hair? Do nuns have hair?'

'I do,' I said. 'I suppose some do, some don't. What does it matter since it doesn't show?'

'But I thought they cut off your hair when you were becoming a nun?'

'Some Orders do. We just have to have it neat enough to fit under our bonnets.'

'So! The headgear!' said Maeve. 'Our veils consist of three separate bits. The white cotton bonnet which covers the head and is drawn in and can be tightened around the face by pulling the strings inside the bottom and a little of the sides.'

Our Pat was now standing on the bench so that she could have a good look at Sister Maeve's veil.

'On top of this bonnet is a starched band to go around the forehead, with a bit at the top that isn't starched so that it can be drawn in with two tiny strings around the head. The black veil that goes over all of this is simply attached to it by pins. The veil is made from two pieces of special quality black material carefully sewn together to take the shape of the head and, as one can clearly see, hangs loosely over one's shoulders and down one's back just covering the cape.'

No photos were taken that day but I can still see Pat peering under Maeve's veil as Maeve explained all these intricacies. And I have my own pictures in my head of all of us trying to walk around in a dignified manner on a very hot day in long black habits made of a heavy material.

Later that evening after our parents had left us and we had tidied everywhere, had an evening snack and recited Vespers and Compline, we seven newly professed Sisters observed the custom of placing our crowns around the statue of Our Lady in chapel. We stayed to pray in silence before going to bed.

Because the house was overcrowded with all the extra nuns who had come for the profession ceremonies, our group had to sleep in what had been a greenhouse. It was a hot night and the temperature was high in there. I couldn't sleep so later that night I took a pair of scissors into the toilet and hacked most of my hair off.

That was the August before my twenty-first birthday.

8

Honeymoon

As the weeks went by I felt very sad at being separated from Maeve. She was dispatched to help out with youth work in our Battersea club. My other companions were sent to various destinations but I remained in Friar Park and was assigned to a nearby school to try out my ability in teaching. My parents were to visit on the nearest Sunday to my twenty-first birthday but, because the nuns kept feast-days rather than birthdays, I expected that it would be a muted affair. However, I was no longer under the strict jurisdiction of my novice mistress and I soon discovered that my dear old Sister Superior was prepared to let me celebrate this special birthday by lighting the candles on the cake that my dad's friends at work had sent for the occasion. What's more she brought some of the Sisters into the parlour, where I sat with my parents, to indulge themselves in afternoon tea from the good china cups and a slice of the said cake.

★ ★ ★

'Baby Jesus wants you to go to Africa, Sister Marion. Are you ready?' That's how Mother Provincial asked me if I still wanted to be a missionary.

Because there was need for a Sister to be sent to our house in Cape Town, South Africa, that Christmas Eve I was taken down to a photographer in Henley town to have a passport photo taken.

All over Christmas I kept imagining what it would be like to be far away out in a very hot country, but then I had always wanted to save souls out in darkest Africa. There were lots of farewells and tears shed. I even wrote a goodbye letter to my parents but in the end I was told I would not be going to Africa. I discovered much later on that the Sisters in Cape Town had to move out of their house because the house was haunted! There was a great deal of hush-hush about this initially but eventually I learnt that the Sisters were frightened by strange happenings like typewriters typing on their own, stockings mysteriously slipping down off rails and very loud bangs. The Superiors had to have the house exorcised and some of the nuns who were not believed in the beginning were moved or sent back to England. Eventually they closed the house and the block was razed to the ground and used as a car park, but even then there continued to be strange happenings.

So I was sent to South Farnborough instead of South Africa. One of our Sisters who taught there had become ill. Then in the September of that year, 1967, I began training to be a teacher at Digby Stuart College, Roehampton, Surrey.

★ ★ ★

'Seeing that you have already been teaching for a while now, how do you find the course?' asked my brother Tim when I showed him round the college. He had been visiting a friend in St Mary's Hospital across the road.

'Well, all five of us have been told what subjects to study and the age group we are to train for. I love geography but I've been told to take history because there's a shortage of teachers for that subject in our convents. Sister Elizabeth is to follow the English course but she is mad about art. That's the same for all of us but I suppose we're the fortunate ones. Many of our nuns would love to be us.'

'Any chance of us going inside for a bit? Only I'm tired after that long bus journey up here this afternoon and, on top of that, walking round the hospital to find Jim.'

'There are some chairs there in the entrance. Let's perch ourselves there for a while and watch the world go by.'

'Gee — look at that nun over there — her habit is even more cumbersome and complicated than yours!'

'Well, the Salesian habits are simple compared to many — and not so much material used in them. All to do with John Bosco's concept, I suppose, of our being an active order working close to the laity and our being involved in youth work. You couldn't play many street games in a habit like that nun's! Mind you, nowadays it seems strange that we have to wear habits at all when we do PE and play games. Got to keep ourselves covered.'

'Ridiculous!'

'But, you know, things are changing. Some Orders are beginning to simplify the habit and wear more modern clothes. In fact, don't turn round now but there's a nun coming through the door and you'd hardly know she is one, if you get me.'

'Tell me — you said you nuns have a separate refectory — but, apart from that, are you allowed to mix with the other women in this college?'

'Are you kidding? Salesian Sisters are told not to talk to or mix even with other nuns!'

'Why?'

'Sometimes I think we're made to feel we're a cut above the rest. I don't know, but we're told that we have to save seats for each other and arrive at a fixed time for our lunch in the refectory so that we can sit together and then go for a constitutional walk around the lake and finish up in chapel making what our prayer book calls our 'Visit to the Blessed Sacrament.''

'Sounds as though you're being protected. A bit weird and unchristian though, don't you think?'

'It is. Why should there be rivalry between the various religious Orders? After all, aren't we all out to save souls?'

'That's what you keep telling me. When are you being collected tonight?'

I got up to look at a nearby clock. 'It's almost five already. The others should be here any minute now. Mr Kirkby will drive us home as usual.' As I sat down again nearer to Tim, I whispered, 'When we travel home by minibus we are forbidden to talk to Mr Kirkby or to each other. Then when we go into the convent, if Mother Provincial is in her room, we have to file in, in front of her, and answer any questions she chooses to put to us. After that she'll look into our eyes and tell us if Jesus is pleased with us.'

'And is He?'

'Sorry, can't answer. Here they come. Have to say goodbye now. You'll be OK to find your way home, Tim?'

My brother was an alcoholic although he would not admit that. I worried about him and prayed for him all the time. Eventually his addiction shortened his life. But, luckily perhaps, we can't see what the future holds for any of us.

And little did I know then but the nun Tim had noticed, wrapped in that black habit, three years later emerged from college in a scarlet-red low-cut shirt-waister.

9

Disillusionment

Once a year we were permitted to go home to our parents for a week. Mine had moved back to Ireland for the second time. Mam was in search of happiness again. The rule about us Sisters always travelling in twos had been relaxed. Six years earlier when I was still an aspirant, I had to travel with my five-year-old sister in order to satisfy the stipulation that we were not to travel alone. I was to stay at the local convent, Fernbank, Limerick, and go to my parents each day. Fortunately the Irish Salesian Sisters often allowed me to borrow the community car.

★   ★   ★

One of the Traveller's dogs must have woken me up. My parents were still snoring off the Sunday roast. No wonder the relatives hardly ever came to see them in this rundown part of O'Malley Park, Limerick. Their barely adequate pebble-dashed bungalow looked out onto a hillock of green where the Travellers' horses and dogs roamed at will.

'Will you leave those! The washing-up is Dad's job.'

Mam clicked her lighter so now cigarette smoke would mingle with the dinner smells.

As I ran the water I opened the window and Dad came to life with: 'The fairies are here again! You're a great girl, do you know that?'

I had my back turned to them when I said, 'Sister Sheila's parents are celebrating their silver wedding anniversary this September. You never mention your wedding anniversary. When is it anyway?'

No one replied.

After what seemed ages, Mam asked, her voice sounding strange and forced: 'Have you never looked at your birth cert and our wedding one?'

I turned round to look at Mam.

'I've never . . . no, we don't see them. Why?'

'Well, you see, we were married by the time you were born, but well, not . . . not when you were . . . well . . . well, that's as it is. I thought you knew. I hope you don't think any the less of us. We've tried to do our best.'

I wanted to be sick. I removed my glasses and held onto the sink. What was she saying?

But I heard myself replying: 'Oh! Well, of

course. What does it matter?'

That was how I found out that I was conceived before my parents married.

Into my head flashed something one of the older nuns had told me — that the Holy Rule of the Order said something like: '*Only in exceptional circumstances shall a candidate born outside wedlock be accepted into the Order.*' I had wondered at the time if she was perhaps referring to an already outdated rule — there had been many changes in Canon Law relating to such subjects in 1917. But, now, in my shock and dismay, I forgot such doubts: as far as I was concerned, I had entered the convent under false pretences.

I turned back and clutched the cutlery. I pushed the window further out and scoured the casserole dish with great gusto in an effort to shake off my dizziness. My heart seemed to be dropping down inside my body.

Mam's puckered face told me that she knew I had been dealt a blow but as usual Dad was unaware of the shock I had felt at this revelation. I pretended that I was in control until I reached the bathroom and howled as I flushed the toilet.

When I emerged Mam asked, 'Would you like to go swimming tomorrow, Marion?'

'I'd love to but I have to go back to the convent now.'

★ ★ ★

The convent was in semi-darkness. I desperately wanted to talk to Sister Sheila. Sheila had been a novice with me and later had been moved back to Fernbank. I almost ran up to her room but her light was out. I spent the night questioning and querying things. Five in the morning found me in the bathroom vigorously washing myself. I wanted to bang everything in sight but I was aware that silence before Mass had to be respected. Was I scrubbing off my past?

Determined to keep in control, I drove round to my parents' house. They were ready to go and, unusually, my mother had everything ready for our day out.

'Isn't it a gorgeous day?' Mam said chattily. 'Shall we head off out now and make a day of it? Aren't we lucky that the nuns have let us have the car again? They're very good to us but you work hard too and Dad and I are very proud of you, you know that? Sure I carry your photo round in my bag all the time.'

I couldn't bear her forced cheeriness, now that I understood at last what had been tormenting her all these years.

★ ★ ★

'I can't swim for much longer. Hold on! I think the nun's moving towards the car.'

'I'll have to get out no matter what, Mam. I'm really cold now.'

There we were out in Ringmoylan kicking, hitting and splashing the sea water captured in a swimming-pool. Normally I loved this place but I hated it that day. I wanted to scream. I couldn't look my mother in the eyes. I was bursting out of my skin and pretending all was fine.

Dad was calmly walking round the pool. How could he? Didn't he realise that I'd been trapped? Deceived? It was while I was battling with my feelings that the car pulled up. Dad called out, 'One of the nuns is after coming!'

I looked over and there was Sister Bridie and her family settling themselves down on a bench a stone's throw away from us. This was all I needed! Being discovered in my swimsuit! We were not permitted to take off our habits so what would she think of me in this state?

'I'll have to take a chance. Maybe as I'm over from England she may not recognise me.'

And that's what happened. Mam and I walked right by Sister Bridie and she said hello and carried on talking. This was the first year I had begun disobeying orders and taking off my habit to go for a swim. On these occasions I also went to Mass and recited the Office in lay clothes, but I used to hope that if any of the Irish nuns saw me they wouldn't recognise me.

★　★　★

'Oh, my God, you look worried, Sister Marion! Are your parents all right?'

'Sheila, I feel sick. I feel as though the bottom has fallen out of my life and I want to collapse. No, I want to be put to sleep and not woken up until . . . I don't know what to do!'

'Good God, what's happened? Come in here to the refectory. The Sisters are in chapel. Now let me get you — have you eaten?'

'No, but it's not food that I need.' Tears began to dribble down my cheeks. I pulled a tissue out of my pocket with one hand and lowered my head to rest on the other.

'In the name of God, what's happened? Has someone died?'

Sheila had pushed her chair up to mine and placed her arm round my shoulders. I was shaking.

Between the sobs I spluttered: 'Why was I

never told that I am illegitimate? Why? Why? Sheila, I shouldn't be in the convent at all! I'm contaminated goods! I have just discovered that I was conceived outside wedlock and you know what the Rule says about that! Me, Preachy Miss Perfect, shouldn't have been accepted! Should not have been professed!' I pushed Sheila back from holding me.

She smiled at me and put an arm about me again. 'Marion! That's nonsense! You're a love child! Doesn't that make you special? And did you not just say *conceived* outside wedlock?'

'Yes!' I sobbed.

'But then you're not illegitimate! Your parents were married when you were born! And even if you *were* illegitimate, so what?'

'But the Rule!'

'I've never heard anything about such a rule — it sounds so outdated — are you sure it still exists?'

'What difference does it make? I'm wrong! I'm an exception! I'm no good to anyone, am I? How can I be telling people to do things right and all the time I'm false, impure! Contaminated!'

'Hold on there. How do you make that out? *You* weren't responsible!'

'I made my final vows two years ago,' I

sobbed. 'I'll be thirty this September. I spent last night going over all those years — and to think, well, what am I? You know what I am. I'm my mother's sin offering! That's what I am. Like they did in the Bible, she offered me to God — to placate the Almighty — to pay Him back for the sin she had committed!'

'Marion, you're going to make yourself sick with all this anger. Listen, there'll be no one in the parlour this time of night. Will we go in there? While you go in I'll put a hot drink on for myself and, do you know, I think a drop of wine wouldn't do you any harm. Will you have a small drop? I know where there's some.'

Hours later I was still saying, 'I'm my mother's sin offering, that's what I am.'

The other nuns must have all taken themselves off to bed.

'Now I know why my mother went in to see Sister Superior privately when I first entered the *aspirantade*. No doubt they were negotiating my future! Examining my birth certificate!'

'I'm sure that's not true. Why would your mother tell Sister Superior anything about that?'

'Because my mother has been carrying a burden of guilt since I was conceived! But, what I want to know is — what say did I have

94

in all of this? I was traded off in exchange for forgiveness for my mother's sin! I mean, I was being used as cheap labour in the *aspirantade* for four years!'

'But so were we all, Marion.'

'Do you know, it's all coming back to me now! I was actually told I'd be sent home after I complained one day.'

'Why was that?'

'I'll never forget it. We, the aspirants, had to stay in school after the day students went home. That was so awful! They'd almost trip over us on the stairs in our overalls with our brushes and dustpans and what's more we weren't permitted to even talk to them! Well, anyway, this wintry afternoon Pat O' and myself were pushing a homemade wooden effort across the hockey field which separated the school from the house. The cart was heavy with the leftovers from the school dinners and a huge jug filled with the remains of the thirds-of-a-pint bottles of milk. This lot would be warmed up for our evening meal. We hated this and we also resented having to push it over the field.'

'I can imagine a crocodile of six or eight of you exhausted craturs trudging home. We had tough times here in Ireland but we were spared the likes of that.'

'We were supposed to keep the silence on

this journey. But I took a fit of laughter. I don't remember what triggered it off but Sister Hilda poked me in the back. Well, that did it. I laughed out loud and what's more all the rest joined in. She then told me that if I continued I'd be sent home and find my case outside on the landing that very same night!'

'That seems out of all proportion to the crime.'

'That's what I think now. Were they waiting for me to break out?'

'Oh, I really don't think so! You know how tough the discipline was for all of us! Sister Hilda might have been having a bad day!'

'I wish now I had been sent home then, you know.'

'You've been bottling this up for ages, haven't you, Marion?'

'Sheila, I have been so lonely and trying to struggle with my feelings and wondering if others felt the same. I have asked repeatedly why I have found things so hard. I resented, for example, not being allowed to hold my little sister in my arms when my mam brought her to the convent soon after she was born.'

'Well, you know that was because the Sisters didn't want you to go broody?'

'But I have always loved children. Over the years when I was teaching, every time I listened to the children practising their reading, I longed to cuddle them. Is there something lacking in me? Sheila, have you felt like that?'

'Yes, we're women, aren't we? Most women want children. No, I wouldn't torture yourself for having natural motherly feelings. What use would you be without them?'

'But I still feel cheated! There I was aged fourteen being farmed off to the convent because my mother felt guilty. Yes, I know I wanted to go. But over the years I'd been brainwashed into thinking that God called me to be a nun! Then I go along and work like a Trojan, eat reheated or out-of-date food, say reams of prayers and beat myself for my impure inclinations and all for what? I just feel like shooting the lot of them!'

'You just made your perpetual vows, Marion. Nobody forced you to do that. Why don't you just forgive your mother and also consider that life outside the convent can't be that easy?'

Eventually I apologised for keeping Sister Sheila up so late but as I tried to sleep that night I wondered if I would be better off living as a lay person. Maybe if I left now I would be able to marry and have children. But then I'd remember that my family would never be able to help me. How could they?

Weren't they often asking the nuns to help them? Maybe many of the nuns felt trapped like me, too. Was that why a few Sisters had been keeping back some of the change from the shopping they had been sent on and when they had enough they had bought themselves underwear and nightdresses and other things like clocks and even mirrors? Then there were others that had rich relatives who gave them presents and they were allowed to keep these even though they were not supposed to. Some Sisters also wanted to study and when refused had become unhappy and others had left and not even been allowed to say goodbye.

I felt so unloved and lonely and I longed to be loved.

I asked myself too why it was that the priests seemed to be able to go where they liked and live as they liked and were much freer than us nuns.

I fell asleep that night with these words of Sister Sheila's burrowing into my head:

'You don't seem as happy as you used to be. What's happening to you?'

10

Flashes and Flushes

'I hope you don't mind but earlier while you were getting ready for our walk I read the copy of your CV that was here on the table.'

'Not at all. I left it there so that we could catch up.'

Valerie Wells, my old school friend, now married with two sons, had come to visit me. 'By the looks of it you seem to have been chucked out of lots of schools!'

'Now, now, Valerie! I'll have you know that I have taken a vow of obedience and I get marching orders every time a vacancy crops up in any of our houses. But I know what you mean. I admit it seems as if I lack staying power or else I've got problems big-time!'

'It's so Catholic too! Our Lady's First School Chertsey, St Bernard's Glasgow and the Sacred Heart Battersea!'

'Well, I *am* a nun, you know.'

'Yes, I do know! And I was so glad that you were allowed to join us at our past pupils' reunion! I was delighted that Sister Philomena and Sister Mary of the Sacred Heart were there. Shame they've had to sell the school though. Tooting Broadway has changed so much.'

Valerie swayed back and forth on the rocking-chair that one of our nuns' relatives had recently donated to our convent in Eastworth Road, Chertsey. We were relaxing after a long walk through the broken bracken torn by the January winds.

'Thanks for letting me come to visit you,' she said now. 'It was difficult to speak at the reunion with everyone recapping their lives in such loud voices, wasn't it?'

'Impossible!'

'But, Marion, I just can't believe that you never received all the letters I wrote to you way back all those years ago . . . it was after I came to visit you that time — '

'Yes. Did you ever forgive me for telling the Sister Superior that you were thinking of joining up with the nuns?' I laughed.

'No, I didn't! There I was down to say hello to my school friend and I found myself in the parlour being asked when I had heard God calling me to help the Sisters to save souls! I mean, fancy dropping me in it like that!'

'Well, can you take it as a compliment? You see, I missed you so much and I did want to save the world and I thought you'd be good at that!'

Valerie laughed. 'Oh well, lots of water has gone under the bridge! Maybe I should forgive you! But what I still can't understand is why your letters were censored — I mean, not given to you? There was nothing scandalous in them. I even asked our Holy Family nuns at school if they could explain why I virtually had been cut off from you. Our friendship was severed so abruptly.'

I sighed. 'They thought they were protecting me from 'the world'.'

Valerie stretched her hand out and took mine. She pursed her lips as she exclaimed, 'Never mind! Let's not waste the time we have today. It's funny how we both ended up as teachers, isn't it?'

'I love teaching, Valerie, do you? It's like being on the stage acting, entertaining, at the same time as honing in to discover what makes each child tick and lead them on to the next step in their learning process.'

'Well, I suppose that's why we stick it out!'

'I remember when one of my early pupils, little Cathy, matched her name card to the one on her locker and shouted out, 'Look, Sister, that's my name! I can read!' I shared her wonderment.'

'Times like that are magic, aren't they?'

'I know. Only this morning a five-year-old boy in my class called Richard flung his arms

101

round me in the playground and I wanted to hug him!'

'You must wish you had children of your own, Marion?'

'Yes. Sometimes I wonder what's happening to me. Take for instance when Mrs Cain told me that I was not distant like the other nuns . . . '

We were silent for a while as she scanned my CV again

'Tell me — what was it like in Scotland?' she asked then.

'I loved it up there! We were five in the community in Paisley and two of us taught in Glasgow. St Bernard's school was excellent. Very sociable too because Mr Devlin used to expect each member of the staff to have a party piece to entertain the others at the many social gatherings we had — out of school hours of course!'

'And what was it like in such a small community?'

'Again it was good. Although we observed the timetable we were not slaves to it and so were able to be more relaxed and supportive of each other. We allowed ourselves time to bond and reminisce. We had some good laughs when we talked about how strict it was in the noviciate. In fact, whenever we mentioned Signora Maestra someone would shout out, 'DT!' which stood for 'Dangerous Topic'!'

'That sounds like a healthy approach!'

Eventually the talk shifted to my family. When I told her that I was forever preaching and advising my brothers and sisters as to how they should live she called me 'Bossy Boots' but she shed a tear with me when I related what had happened to my brother Tim. I had suggested to him that he should give up the drink and get a job. On the very next Monday he'd drilled through an electric cable out on a busy road in White City and was rushed by ambulance to the burns unit in Billericay Hospital with eighty per cent burns. The headmistress released me from teaching and Sister Superior loaned me the community car to drive to him immediately, but I couldn't forgive myself for shortening his already damaged life. (He never really recovered and never worked again but continued to drink, sadly dying at the age of fifty-seven.)

From Tim we moved to talk about my mother.

'What was it about her that made her suffer so much?' asked Valerie.

Initially I was too embarrassed to tell her the truth I had discovered about my birth but eventually I managed to tell her the story.

'But I don't understand why that should distress you so badly!' she said.

'Well, it's just that at first I was so sure that the Rule stated a candidate could not be accepted if she was conceived outside wedlock — '

'You do realise that half the population or even more fall into the 'conceived outside wedlock' category, don't you?'

'I know that now! But I didn't then! In any case, I had that wrong — it was *born* outside wedlock, not *conceived* outside wedlock — and, you know, I can't find any mention of it in the latest copy of the Constitutions. But all I know is that we had to be near perfect, purer than white, and once my mother admitted that I was 'conceived outside wedlock' I felt that I was contaminated goods. So there I was, preaching to others, telling them how to live! Then I was knocked off my pedestal! I felt humiliated and unfit, disappointed, a fraud, dirty and horrible.'

Try as I might I couldn't explain to Valerie why I felt so disappointed with myself when I discovered that I was my mother's 'sin offering'. What's more, I knew that it still mattered to me. Nor did I tell her that I was so ashamed that I did not broach the subject with any of those in authority. Nor that I wondered if I would eventually have to leave the Order, I felt so ill at ease. And I didn't tell her how scared I felt at even the thought that I might ever have to return to the outside world that I had left aged fourteen.

'I see, Clever Clogs, that you got your degree!' Valerie broke in on my pondering.

'Oh, yes, my Bachelor of Education handed to me by no less than Her Majesty Queen Elizabeth The Queen Mother herself in The Royal Albert Hall on 9th May 1979! Mam in a baby blue suit and Dad with his tweeds on, proud as peacocks. Caps, gowns, applause, congratulations and Mam saying as we left: 'Do you know what I noticed, Marion? There was a definite pause before they read out your name.' And Dad spluttering, 'Ah, come on now, Patsy, you're imagining things!' And then didn't we almost step off the kerb in front of the Royal car! Mam exclaimed, 'Jesus, will you look? Isn't that the Queen Mother being driven out?' And Dad said: 'Isn't it as well she didn't know about your Uncle Michael being in the IRA, Patsy?''

'That was a day to remember!' said Valerie, laughing.

'It was a lovely day,' I sighed, remembering how we crossed the busy road to marvel at the images of the great Dante Alighieri on the Prince Albert Memorial. Dad was in his element.

We had tea and I showed her some photos. As I eventually got up to put our teacups on to a tray, Valerie stood up to give me a big hug, saying as she did, 'I think I know you better now, Marion. God, what a lot of pathos alongside humour and longing! You were so honest with your nuns about how you felt. It's all very human, you know? Thank you for sharing so much with me. I feel privileged to get a glimpse into how it was and maybe still is, for you.'

'Oh, Valerie, thank you for being there. It's not everyone I feel I can tell about a life that is not remarkable . . . but just different . . . '

★　★　★

But I had not told Valerie everything. I had not told her about my second stint in Chertsey from 1984 to '87. And Father Mike.

During that period of my life the nagging and doubting surfaced even more, though I tried desperately hard to throw myself into my teaching and parish work. I learnt how to play the guitar and helped organise the folk group in the local parish. And whenever I was depressed and lonely I could rely on the kindness of Sisters Bridget and Anne in the kitchen and laundry. I could rely on them to feed and listen to me and be supportive no matter what happened to me or when my family continued to be needy and call for help.

We ran the parish prayer group in the front room of our convent every Tuesday evening and Father Mike often chose the hymns that he accompanied on his guitar. While anyone was welcome to join, it was very rarely any of the Sisters did. So on most nights there were only six or seven ordinary folk and Father Mike and myself, listening to a part of scripture or something else inspirational, and applying it to what was happening to us in our lives. Father Mike or any of us might voice our interpretation of the passage that had been read. Or we could choose to share our feelings or fears aloud in a prayer to the Almighty. Sometimes people had worries or concerns that they wanted to unravel in the privacy of the group or else, with closed eyes, we might pray silently. Anyone who felt inspired could come out with an exclamation or phrase or ask Father Mike to intone a hymn.

I loved participating in that prayer group because I had always enjoyed singing and also it allowed me to do something with adults I enjoyed being with. I had taught their children years before and they had often invited my family around to their houses. A good deal of trust and acceptance had been built up between us so that we were freed to share our feelings and express ourselves without fear.

But I loved that prayer group too because when Father Mike plucked his guitar I was mesmerised and his husky voice excited me. He oozed with music from his crown to his tapping toes and plucked those guitar strings with such sensitivity that my spirits rose and I dreamed of everlasting love and harmonious happiness.

It would have been obvious to everyone in the Prayer Group that I was in love with this sturdy hulk of a priest with his lilting northern accent. Like my father, he was a fine cut of a man, six foot and more, with bristling greying curls and laughing deep-opal marine eyes.

Yes, I fell in love with him and I didn't really hide it. In fact we joked about this being the case and the women in the group told their husbands that they loved him too.

I began to bring my guitar along on a Tuesday night to be tuned by Father Mike and as the prayer group left the convent long after the Sisters had gone to their rooms I was responsible for locking up the back door. But before that, I would have to close the big gates that led into the grounds. So most evenings, after we had all hugged each other goodnight and they had all driven off, I would walk Father Mike out to the gate. He would help me bolt it, we would linger and talk, and then I looked forward to my final big hug and kiss.

Little did I know that, for many years to come, my one comfort would be to relive the wonderful sensations I experienced then, when Father Mike held me in his strong all-embracing arms. I could feel his stubbled face against mine and smell the tweedy fibres from his woolly jacket and the throbbing of his loving heart as we moved closer and closer in the dark near the convent gates. I didn't feel guilty about it because, each time I told Father Mike that I loved him, he reminded me that it was Jesus we both really loved through each other and the more we loved each other the more we loved Jesus. So I hugged him tighter and he told me I was doing him good by showing him that I supported him in his difficult mission working with teenagers in the parish.

Yes, it is a mercy that we cannot foresee the future. Some years after that, my beloved Father Mike was involved in a car accident which left him somewhat changed in character. He suffered from depression but none the less was made parish priest and the parish loved him. He continued to sing and even started up a new group of religious that lived in a house together.

When he died three years ago, there were so many people that they had to move the venue to a bigger church. I had gone to see him at the nursing home but arrived to find him asleep. I kissed him goodbye and went to his funeral soon after.

We had not kept up contact in later years. In fact, he passed a remark once about my leaving the Order that gave me the impression that he did not approve. I think that he genuinely considered that he was loving Jesus in me and that I was doing the same. Did he ever feel guilt? It didn't seem he did. I later thought I had succumbed to this attraction because of an inbred flaw in me. I was a love child after all.

11

Crisis

'I want to throw open the windows of the Church so that we can see out and the people can see in.'

That's what our lovely smiley Pope John XXIII said in 1981. He was responsible for calling the Second Vatican Council which took place from 1962 to 1965. It had a big impact on every aspect of the Catholic Church's approach on everything but naturally renewal took a long time before it really affected most of us. In fact, many ordinary folk only came to realise some of the consequences of these changes when local priests were instructed to celebrate the Mass in English instead of Latin and we came to adopt or adapt Church of England hymns. Liturgical hymn-singing courses run by Kevin Mayhew Publishers of Music were well attended. Guitars, flutes and even tambourines replaced organs in accompanying folk music. Those who studied Theology or were engaged in religious education took part in

111

debates and discussions in centres like Corpus Christi College in London where some famous theologians who had left the priesthood ran courses. Lots of new thinking emerged from that college which caused a bit of scandal and some of the Superiors refused to let their nuns follow these courses. Some of our nuns and priests began to bring some radical ideas and theories back into our communities.

Constitutions, Rule Books and Manuals in Religious Orders had to be updated too. Meetings were held at all levels to ensure that from the grass roots up all were involved. As with others, our Order wanted to recapture its original charisma.

The motto 'Da mihi animas, cetera tolle' ('Give me souls, take away everything else') led Don Bosco and Mother Mazzarello to inspire us 'to dedicate ourselves to the little and poor ones as the soul for our educative mission'.

That quotation and the one below taken from the Constitutions and Regulations (Rome 5th August 1982) encouraged us Sisters to look again at how our apostolate had developed:

'Our Rule urges us to go out to children and young girls of the working classes, *especially the poorest . . . to keep alive the missionary fervour of our origins . . . in the local Churches.'*

My brother Des thought he was bringing me down to earth when he said: 'You should come here to the East End of London and work in tough schools instead of teaching in posh areas like Chertsey. You told me that John Bosco, or is it 'Don' Bosco you call him? Whatever! You said he was out for helping the really poor. It's down here in the likes of Walworth or round the Elephant and Castle that you need to be!'

'That's what I've been shouting out and guess what? Our nuns have bought a house in Rotherhithe and I've volunteered to be moved there. So there!'

Those were very turbulent times for us nuns. During a comparatively short period, the habit we wore changed from being an all-enveloping head-to-toe black garment to becoming a just-below-the-knee length, slimmed-down grey version. What we wore mattered.

'Flesh-coloured stockings are not allowed. Mother Angela distinctly said that on our Retreat,' said Sister Anne.

'Well, I heard it quite clearly stated that we are permitted to wear either flesh-coloured or grey stockings or even tights. Sister Josephine listened when some of the Sisters explained that grey looked much more in keeping with our shorter-length grey habits and I agree with her.'

'What about those who are wearing the new shorter black habits? Holy Poverty prohibits us from discarding these and you know as well as I do that flesh or grey will look out of place with them, Sister Mary!'

'Now, Sisters,' I said, 'let's not get too worked up about the colour of our leg wear! This is the first time I can recall having two different Mother Provincials presiding over two retreats running concurrently. I'm not denying that those of you on one retreat have come away convinced that the outgoing Provincial said that you are to continue wearing grey stockings while those of you on the retreat presided over by our new Provincial believe you can wear flesh-coloured stockings. But remember that we have much more important things than the colour or our stockings to concern us!'

'Forgive me, Sister, but I consider how we interpret the ruling from Rome on these smaller issues to be symptomatic of how the English Province obeys all instructions given from the Mother House on *all* matters.'

And so the discussions continued on issues such as the wearing of bras, because we no longer covered our upper bodies with a cape, having our hair cut properly instead of it being chopped since it was going to be seen and having a coat or anorak replacing our shawls because we often had to travel on London transport instead of by car.

We met various times to discuss the updating of our Constitutions.

'I don't know where we'll end up, Sister!' exclaimed Sister Anne. 'We seem to be going from one extreme to another with our habit! I mean, one minute it's long and body-concealing garb with no foundation garments needed! The next it's like something that could be ordered from a catalogue and bears little resemblance to a nun's habit!'

'You know Jumpy Jacinta? Saint Joseph's Order?' I tried to jog her memory.

'Was she the one whose veil was always lopsided? Was she at the last Catechetical Meeting we went to?'

'The very same. You should have seen the cut of her when they began changing the habit!'

'That's another thing. Some of our nuns are going to look awful when they're not covered up!'

'I was in a group with this Sister Jacinta

when I was asked to lead a discussion group on 'Guilt!'"

'Guilt. Aren't we experts on that subject?' Anne raised her eyes, hands and arms to heaven.

'Well, having attacked the door-handle coming into the room, Sister Jacinta arrived in front of me with the pockets of her long cardigan bulging with all sorts of shapes, looking as though she was going to topple out of her black, down-at-the-heel slip-ons. 'Oh, you're in here!' says she. Then didn't she notice I had the Mass Manual? So she began pointing her finger, outraged that we had removed the Manual from its usual place in the sacristy. I thought she was going to poke my eyes out. She was nearly hysterical. She said, 'What might you be doing with that?''

'Imagine!'

'With that I started off reciting the prayer at the beginning of Mass — the new version in English — '*I confess to Almighty God and to you my brothers and sisters, that I have sinned through my own fault in my thoughts and in my words, in what I have done and in what I have failed to do . . .*''

Well, of course she joined in and I was able to say to her: 'See, Sister Jacinta, sin, going to confession, fault-finding, being in the wrong, are an integral part of our lives.'

* * *

The changes brought about by Pope John XXIII left us feeling excited and bewildered simultaneously.

While I welcomed more feminine underwear and felt it more hygienic to show my hair and wear sandals instead of shoes in the summer, I wanted to remain faithful to serious aspects of our Constitutions like working with the poor. Don Bosco had begun life as a poor boy. My family was poor and needy and so I wanted to save the likes of them.

However, now that we were allowed and even encouraged to think for ourselves, we were becoming more individual in our approach to the way we lived. Our Rotherhithe community of seven had two cars. The headmistress drove the short distance to work. She and others were often absent from some of the community prayers and ate their meals separately. Once we began to become engaged in more social-type work it was more difficult to observe the periods of silence. We watched more television programmes and could provide legitimate excuses for reading novels and books other than the Bible, the Holy Rule and the lives of the saints. That part of the house that would have been the enclosure no longer existed, so the only part ordinary lay people were forbidden to enter was restricted to the bedrooms. Consequently friends, 'Cooperators' and family went into the kitchen and other private rooms.

Another of the meetings attended by roughly a hundred of our nuns to discuss changes in our Rule was held in a Bermondsey school where one of our nuns was headmistress. Financial matters were on the agenda. It was acknowledged then that, although the teachers' salaries paid most of the bills, it had become necessary for Sister Rita Carroll to be assigned extra begging days in some of the London markets.

Mother Provincial, the Sister in charge of our English Province, stood on a rostrum, adjusting her veil before addressing rows of us facing her in a big hall. 'As most of you will be aware, Sister Rita for years has been getting up very early three days a week in order to go to the market and beg for food and other necessities for the ten communities in this country. We are very grateful to you, Sister Rita.'

Many turned round to see a very red-faced Sister Rita pull her veil down as she lowered her head.

Sister Rita used to drive to Covent Garden market in a van and collect or beg for any food that was about to be disposed of. Back at Streatham Convent some of the Sisters would help unload whatever she had obtained: veg, chickens, fish, tins of soup, bread, cake, biscuits etc. Chickens were cleaned, heads chopped off fish, outer dead layers of cabbages cleaned off and so on. The food was then taken down narrow wooden steps to a whitewashed cellar. This was rigged up with lighting and was a labyrinth of passages. Each type of food was stored appropriately, some in fridges. Then, on an appointed day and time, a Sister from another house would drive to Streatham to load up with some of the food. (Flowers were also provided by Sister Rita though a lot of our flowers were returned from funeral parlours by relatives who had their relations cremated and didn't know what to do with the bouquets — the community agreed to pray for the deceased in return for the flowers.)

Begging had gone on in our Province at least since 1959 when I had first joined up and may have been an aspect of Salesian life from the beginning. However, our needs were changing. More nuns were beginning to leave the Order and those who remained were getting older. True, we were selling off bigger houses but the properties we wanted to move into in the cities cost more. We had begun to wear ready-made underwear, cardigans and each of us had a coat rather than a shawl. More of us needed to be trained for youth, social and pastoral work and some of the nuns who had taught in our private-run schools were no longer permitted to continue without recognised qualifications.

'I thought when I made my vow of poverty and signed my Covenant on the day of my profession, I had left all money matters behind me,' I complained to my brother one Sunday when he came to visit me at the convent.

'Well, these meetings might help you all realise what life's like for the rest of us,' Des replied. 'Anyway, what else was in that Covenant thing you signed?'

'All I remember was that a few days after I had made my vows Sister Economer (as we called our bursar) called me into a private room and told me to write over the places on a form that had already been pencilled in. I didn't even understand what I was writing! I was so scared that I even spelt my name with an 'a' because she had written it that way!'

'I hope you realise that, although you may live in a poor area, you will never feel as insecure as we feel.'

'How come?'

'You know that you may be living poor lives but you will never be put out on the street like some of the people round here. Your rent will be paid and if anything happens to one of you, you have a big Order of nuns and priests behind you.'

That was an uncomfortable thought.

12

Breakdown

How could I tell my parents and family that the life I had signed up to was changing so much that I was frightened and confused? I was teaching part-time until a full-time post became available but I knew that the headmistress, Sister Margaret, who belonged to another Order, showed little intention of employing me full-time. Never having worked in a school that was not run by our nuns before, I did not know how to interact with the staff at break or dinner-time. Sister Margaret wore a costume and no veil, but I had to walk a mile to school on my own, feeling that people were pointing me out because I was conspicuous wearing a habit.

At this time I began to pray or just talk aloud to God in a very personal way. Maybe I was forced to cope this way simply because I was too puzzled about my feelings for my friend Sister Maeve and ashamed to admit my utter desperation to any other human.

I felt alienated and longed to be able to turn to her for support. But I had already been warned about getting too close to her.

One weekend around this time Sister Maeve had come over from our Battersea community to deliver an important letter from Mother Provincial to our Sister Superior. I was overjoyed to see her.

'Sister Maeve, there's a book over in the club that I think you might be interested in for ideas about games! Can you spare a minute or two?' The club was run from a building which had a big hall, next to the convent.

Maeve smilingly agreed to go and see the book.

Forgive me, Jesus, but I need to be loved and hugged. I'll collapse otherwise!

Once we got out of sight of the others I flung my arms around Maeve and held her tightly for a few minutes.

'I longed for you to come and was excited when Sister said it was you bringing the letter or whatever it was. Oh, Maeve, I want to be hugged and loved and I'm lonely. What's happening to me?'

'Marion, we are meant to be there for each other but . . . we have been warned so often that we Sisters must not get too dependent on each other. And people notice. For instance, I don't understand why those two Sisters who work in the club absent themselves from community life so often. Does the work in the club necessitate this? Maybe it's just the different timetable has driven them together. I've heard others say that those two are like two peas in the one pod.' She fell silent for a moment. 'I don't know . . . maybe I'm just envious that they are such good friends . . . and can spend time together . . . '

'Yes, that's the nature of their work. And times are changing. But they are lucky. I so much need to see you and to be near you and to have hugs! Oh, can I have one now?'

We hugged again and I wanted to stay longer in her embrace but one of the Sisters went past the window and I felt embarrassed.

'I promise that I will . . . no, I can't do that . . . I love you, Marion, and I feel for you and I look forward to seeing your face and we go back a long way. I know that you're going through a hard time but . . . but we have been warned all the way through our training that special exclusive relationships can destroy community life. Don't look so bedraggled! Come on, give me another hug before we go back! We'll have to or the others will be talking about us!'

We held hands as we walked until we thought we might be seen by others.

Later I wondered if I had clung on to

Maeve too tightly that morning. The thought preyed on my mind.

Anyone who bumped into me when I walked home from school might have heard my grumbling prayer:

'Dear God, why am I so lonely and perpetually tired? I wish I wasn't the only one from our community teaching in that school. If only Sister Maeve could be with me! Is there something wrong with that relationship? But then we have to be careful with special and exclusive friendships. Are people looking at me dressed in my habit? They probably think I'm strange and I am. I should be happy but I'm not. Don Bosco worked non-stop with young people. What's going to become of me? My breath's beginning to smell and I'm losing weight. Something's really wrong with me.'

Reading articles in our Constitutions like the following one only added to my feelings of inadequacy.

Article 58: 'Let us make sure that our houses are always open and welcoming to young people. We shall live our Salesian assistance in constant availability, especially during recreation and in the various leisure activities. The direct contact with young people will enable us to understand better their problems and their values, and so guide them to live according to the Gospel.'

My mother had not changed either. As she aged her depression and sense of guilt seemed to weigh on her. She smoked heavily and had begun to blot out her worries with drink, constantly moving from one flat to another from Brixton to Deptford and Walworth and twice back to Limerick. She was always and often made welcome at the convent where she showed her appreciation and accepted any help that was offered. The trappings of guilt weighed heavy and I seemed to be her trump card.

I was aware that my brothers and sisters were struggling but I too was feeling weak, frail and bewildered. I did not know why I felt so depressed and worried so much about everything. Others in community seemed to have relatives who were able to cope and sometimes gave them gifts or even took them out. Other Orders of nuns were beginning to have pocket money but the mention of that was anathema in our Order where we had to ask for money to buy what was strictly necessary and account for every penny. Some of our nuns had begun experimenting in living in very small communities and in flats.

A few of our Sisters in Ireland were said to have abandoned the habit altogether and to have asked for exclaustration (i.e. living outside the convent) so as to discern if they still had a vocation.

Two of our nuns became so enthusiastic and dedicated to running the youth club that they went to bed very late and hardly took part in the daily timetable of the community but instead of being reprimanded they were commended for their Salesian spirit. But I felt that the life I had joined had changed so that there were very few certainties any more. A good deal of my privacy had been invaded. Alone I was pulled into a quagmire of disillusionment.

Concerned with my condition, the nun in charge often sent me to the doctor and, inevitably, when I walked into the surgery in my grey habit the doctor appeared to regard me as some kind of curiosity and intimated that my condition might be attributable to my lifestyle.

I no longer believed in much of what I was teaching. Bread and wine being changed into the Body and Blood of Jesus. '*Yuk! Yuk! And Frankenstein!*' was what my First Communion class screamed. I questioned everything and was becoming more convinced that God did not really want me to suffer in this life in order to merit eternal bliss.

Please God, forgive me! I can't admit that I've resorted to reading novels and imagining that the love affairs described so vividly in them are happening to me, in order to dull my pain. You created me so you'll know I have to do something to help me survive.

★ ★ ★

I went for my '*rendiconto*', the appointment that each of us had with our Sister Superior after our monthly retreat day which was always on the first Saturday of the month. I knew that I was expected to give some account of myself and how I was getting on in the community, and equally the Superior had the responsibility of making her observations and recommendations known about how she saw my contribution and behaviour. As Rule 34 of the Constitution states:

> '*An especially valuable occasion for strengthening sisterly union, discovering God's will and deepening the spirit of the Institute at a practical level, is the personal meeting that each Sister will have with her Superior. This meeting will take place monthly, in an atmosphere of faith and charity, mutual trust,*

sincerity and secrecy.'

After she welcomed me and I sat myself on the other side of her desk, she enquired:

'Marion, you and I have always been able to be frank and open with each other, have we not?' Then she laughed.

I smiled but nervously wondered what she was hinting at.

'We all have our worries and I know you have had your share but I like to think that we can discuss anything here where it should be said. That's why I'm here, isn't it? If we go to each other to unburden ourselves, well, the other Sister will have our load as well as her own. Our crosses are made to fit our shoulders, aren't they? So while we can be friends with each other no sister should become too dependent on another.'

I felt a sudden surge of heat through my body and the palms of my hands were perspiring. Was I being reprimanded? Surely Maeve would not have said anything about me confiding in her?

I let Sister Superior continue.

'Sometimes we have to safeguard ourselves. For our own sanity's sake it might become necessary to disclose things to someone in authority.'

I let out an 'Oh!'

'Naturally confidentially prevents me from releasing any names but I want you to remember why in our Salesian way of life we have always been warned against special relationships. As you know this kind of friendship can only lead to disaster. Sisters in the community only report any observations they have in order to nip these relationships in the bud.'

There was a long pause as she scrutinised my facial expression. I could feel I had gone red. I removed and cleaned my glasses a few times. What had Maeve said? Had she told? Maybe though it was the Sister who passed the window when we were hugging? If only I knew who that was. After all, Maeve had hugged me too! But did she feel guilty? Was this intimacy all too much for her?

I realised that I could not ask any questions. I would just have to accept that I had been warned. All I could do was be careful not to be alone with Maeve again. It was more important to stay friends with her than to spoil all those years we had shared together.

When I next met Maeve there were no hugs although she was friendly and acted as though nothing had happened. I preferred to think that she had been warned too. And I knew, if she *had* said anything to Sister

Superior, it was because she thought it was for the good of both of us. That did not stop me from feeling frustrated and even more lonely, and deprived of having someone all to myself to confide in. And I couldn't help feeling a little betrayed.

★　★　★

One afternoon in 1986, making my way from school to the convent I could barely drag leaden feet behind me. Towering grey concrete London buildings seemed to loom over me like monsters blocking out any source of light and life and I wanted to collapse onto the kerb or better the road and let any bus roll over me.

Eventually I reached the convent, held on to the doorhandle, levered myself in and made for the phone cubicle. I knew Mother Provincial was visiting our Parish Priest. He handed her the phone at once and I managed to tell her that I felt that I couldn't go on any longer. She promised that she would be with me within the hour.

My voice must have betrayed my need because minutes after the doorbell rang and, as I was the only one in, I went out to meet Mother Provincial.

'I'm so sorry . . . I . . . I just don't know

what to do,' I said, stumbling through the words.

She put her arm around my waist, led me into the front room and sat me down in an armchair. When she was sure that there was no one around to listen in, she positioned herself opposite me.

I cried and cried and cried while she supplied me with tissues, repeating 'Just let it come. Don't worry.'

Eventually I was able to tell her how black and miserable and unfit I was to carry on. She listened and sympathised. I felt as weak as if I had the 'flu and I could barely see out of my steamed-up glasses. She asked me what I wanted to do and I didn't know. She suggested I get some help from a doctor. I told her I had seen the doctor and he blamed the way I felt on the type of life I was leading.

'Mother Provincial, it may sound . . . well, do you think the fact that my mother suffers from depression . . . could it be? Might that account in part for why I feel so very low?'

'Marion, you know as much as I do about these things. Do we inherit depression? The fact that your poor mother has always been inclined that way can't be easy for any of the family but you are your own person.'

'I can't thank you enough for all that is done for my family — so much!' I sobbed again and took off my glasses and wiped them and replaced them and tried to smile even though I couldn't focus.

'Where's there an off-licence round here?'

'I've never noticed.'

'Do you feel well enough to come in the car with me? If you are, I'll get you a bottle of Advocaat. Have you ever had that before? It's like *zabaglione*. A mixture of wine and egg. A real good buck-me-up. Would you try that?'

In the course of the next few months I cried through several meetings like this one and was given many bottles of egg-flip.

But even though my tale of woe was listened to, I did not seem to be able to shake off my depression.

Eventually Mother Provincial suggested that I have a complete break in my home country of Ireland. I agreed to give it a try and signed up to do a Pastoral Course in Maynooth, County Kildare.

13

Maynooth

With '*Céad míle fáilte!*' and 'You're very welcome in our house, or rather hostel, Marion!' Sister Margaret received me in Ausilia Hostel in Maynooth to begin a Pastoral Theology course run in St Patrick's Pontifical College. Hearing her Cork lilt made my own Irish accent return as if by magic.

I knew Sister Margaret of course. When I went home to Ireland to see my parents I sometimes made my retreat with the Irish branch of the Province in a big house the Order had in Brosna, County Offaly.

'Thanks, Sister Superior, I'm delighted to be back on home soil at last.'

'Sure, you're more than welcome. But as for the 'superior' bit — well now, we're all on the same level here. It's just that if anything should ever go wrong and there's anyone to blame, that'll be me. How was the journey? I'm sorry there was no one to meet you.'

'I was fine. Once I landed at Dublin airport, just fingering Irish money with horses 'nd hens instead of the Queen's head — well! And coins with a pig and the word 'pig' being 'muc' in Irish! And then the accent! Just to hear the accent tickles me all over.'

'Leave your cases down there now and join us. You've arrived in time for a bite to eat.'

When I was shown into the dining room, I was introduced to the other seven Sisters in the community and in no time was seated round the table tucking into roast meat, potatoes, cauliflower and much more besides. We chatted a good deal too.

While the others washed up Sister Margaret led me upstairs, each of us hauling one of my cases.

'You're in luck because this big front room has just been done up. Built-in wardrobe, rosy bedspread and matching curtains, sink, the lot! Just as it should be.'

'Thank you! This is so good!' I flung my arms round Sister Margaret.

'Gone are the days when we slept in dormitories! The young ones would never believe it. Up to eighteen of us on iron-framed, candlewick-covered beds and the basin we washed in on a stand at the end separated from our neighbour by a sheety curtain! We weren't allowed to complain about snoring — nor sleepwalking either and a lot of that went on!'

'Do you remember Pat Driscoll saying that all that was private for her was in a locker that was open to inspection once a month on Retreat Days?'

'Oh, don't start me off on Retreat Days! On the first Saturday of each month! We really did take them seriously, didn't we? Remember how our prayer described our dying? *'Beads of sweat on our foreheads and our hair standing stiff'*! And just in case we became attached to anything in this world we were constantly allocated new places in chapel, in the dining room and well, everywhere. Haven't we moved on, Marion?'

★ ★ ★

On that first Monday the five of us nuns from our community who were following the Pastoral Theology course weaved our way past three other big hostels in Maynooth campus. Then we went over the bridge into the grand grounds of St Patrick's Seminary and College.

'How're ye?' and 'How're things?' accompanied by welcoming smiles, nods and winks seemed to be the usual greetings from clerics in black swinging gowns and carrying bundles of books.

One of the Sisters pointed out the big

modern-looking library as she led the way to the 'Aula' or lecture room that was to be ours. It was all set out with inkwell desks and benches of the old type facing a long blackboard. Our shoes clattered on the shiny wooden, planked floor. The other nuns there wore the distinctive habits of their different orders and were old, and there were only three men in the class.

Three nuns in pale blue full-length habits in the front bench turned round to shake hands and introduce themselves to a Sister in white with a black-trimmed scapular and a group of Franciscan nuns in their characteristic brown habits. There was a good-looking nun, dressed in a smart black dress with a frilly collar, going up and down the aisle shaking hands with everybody while an older nun, completely covered from veil to boots, dangling rosary beads hanging from her leather belt, was seated in the corner of the large room. The three men had congregated together in the back desks.

The five of us followed each other into a middle row and introduced ourselves. I surmised that I must be the youngest. After about a quarter of an hour a side door opened and a middle-aged priest, with high colouring and dressed in his soutane, rushed onto the podium.

'No doubt you'll have all introduced yourselves, so I'm Michael O'Flynn and as you'll gather from my accent, I hail from the Kingdom. You're all very welcome! *Dia is Mhuire dhaoibh!*'

I knew that meant 'God and Mary be with you' and that Kerry folk always refer to their county as 'The Kingdom'. My heartbeat quickened.

Later that morning we walked round parts of the well-cultivated grounds, which enclosed a square with buildings designed by Pugin, no less, and said to have been in the Gothic Revival style. Towers, turrets and the remains of a castle give the whole place a very grand feel, while the cobbled stones and small workshops and comradeship in the bookshop and the waves and nods make it feel homely.

For the first time in years I was not ashamed of being Irish. Since the sixties and the renewal of the activities of the IRA on mainland Britain, I'd felt accused of plotting against the Establishment every time another bomb was reported on the national news. Even our nuns didn't understand why I said I was proud of my famous great-uncle Michael Colivet, a TD in the first Dáil, who took part in the Easter Rising and served time in British jails for wanting freedom and a United Ireland. Had I fallen into the trap

138

of becoming 'more Irish than the Irish themselves' and living on a surfeit of nostalgia?

There were forty of us in our class and the majority were missionaries who had spent most of their lives in various parts of Africa and Asia and South America. Many were using this course to get a rest and refuel and train for a kind of retirement employment in their parishes or communities. The exams were optional. There were lectures in a variety of 'ologies' in the morning, musical recitals in the afternoons, and we were free to go for walks, cycle or study for the rest of the day.

One of the three men turned out to be Father Jack Rogers, who lived in the hostel next door to ours. He was very tall and thin and had a mellow voice and a beguiling smile. We became friends immediately and very soon arranged to go off cycling around the country roads discussing more than the weather. He used to call for me after dinner two or three times a week. Sometimes, if he arrived early, he'd wait in and chat to the Sisters while I changed into my shorts. No habit then when I relaxed and I wore a much reduced semblance of one in the community too.

When I was talking about him to Sister Agnes that first week, she teased: 'Aha!

There's a twinkle in your eye! You have a soft spot for him, haven't you? That streak of lightning might have a hold on you!'

Later on in the term Sister Agnes quizzed me with: 'How fond of Jack are you, Marion?'

I felt a blush as I tapped my nose while answering 'Ah now!' and continuing with 'Did I tell you how he proved he cared?'

'No. Tell me all.'

'You know that fussy old priest? Oh, what's his name?'

'Reverend Father Patrick O'Dee to you!' she mocked.

'The very one. That self-same holy fellow shouted at me one day a few weeks ago when I accidentally put my foot on the lawn in front of the priests' quarters. The next minute there was Father Jack standing next to me and, on account of him being well known as the nephew of the famous Bishop of Killaloo, that cranky old priest realized that he couldn't reprimand him. So you see, Father Jack has become my knight in shining armour!' I felt the blood rush up my cheeks again.

'What about all those seminarians in Saint John Bosco's Hostel? I enjoy all their lively liturgies over at their chapel, don't you?'

A male counterpart of our Order lived in the hostel opposite us and we used to go over

140

to them for Mass at least once a week. These young men played their guitars to accompany rousing hymns and their liturgies were lively, thought-provoking and meaningful. Some of them seemed very fervent, most were fun-loving and many fell in love and left. The older priests in that house were more relaxed and open to new ideas. Two of them, about my age, often came over to our house to sing and play their guitars with a group of us. When we sang songs like 'Steal Away' there was many a sly smile and a wink seen.

'Yes,' I replied to Sister Agnes's question about the lively liturgies. 'There is such a big contrast between us nuns and priests living on the campuses and that male-dominated atmosphere over in the houses of residence in St Patrick's, isn't there?' The seminarians in St Patrick's were training to be secular priests (not bound by monastic rules) whereas the various hostels were run by particular Orders that were training their men for work in their own missions. 'A bridge separates us but it seems like it's on a different island in some respects, doesn't it? All those Gregorian Chant liturgies and the musical recitals — well, they're inspiring and their beautifully embroidered vestments are to be admired, along with their floral arrangements, but it's their attitude towards women that leaves much to be desired!' Some of the priests had a way of addressing and answering nuns that gave the impression that we were inferior beings, not to be taken seriously.

The ruling on the habit was relaxing all the time for our Order and so, if we felt it necessary in certain circumstances, we could receive permission to wear grey skirts and either a cardigan or jumper with a white blouse or polo-neck top.

One Saturday morning, when I arrived down for breakfast, I must have looked puzzled at the sight of Sister Claire sitting at table wearing a yellow blouse.

Sister Agnes took one look at me and said, 'Marion, didn't God make blue, red and yellow?'

Time passed far too quickly, in a year I had been granted to discern whether or not I should remain in religious life. By May I was still enjoying myself too much and wanted more. What was I going to say to Mother Provincial when she came over from England to speak to me? I only wore my veil now for solemn occasions, I had been away on holiday, I dressed in ordinary clothes, I enjoyed the company of men, I no longer felt obliged to say the Rosary and other formal prayers and had questioned why it was that community living had become such an integral part of our life as nuns.

'A few of us are meeting in Sister Agnes's room tonight at nine for Irish coffee and you're more than welcome to join us, Marion. But keep it to yourself. We'll dim the lights so no need to knock, just come in,' whispered one of our group.

Agnes had the whiskey, cream, a kettle, mugs, spoons and chocolate biscuits. Being the cook meant she had easy access to these supplies. We had two bedside lamps rigged up on floor level and the window over the door had been blacked out. The five of us sat crossed-legged and leant against the bed or the wall. We talked about everything else and then about the fact that I'd have to make up my mind about my future soon.

* * *

Mother Provincial did come to assess how I had progressed as my time in Maynooth ran out. I did not wear my veil. She did not reprimand me but instead got the Provincial Council to agree that I follow a secretarial course in Dublin. In effect, I was being granted a year of exclaustration.

* * *

Of those who followed the Diploma in Religious Studies only Father Jack and I sat and passed the examinations. I had already moved to the Sisters of Mercy Convent in Baggot Street, Dublin, the September before the graduation ceremony in order to follow a secretarial course in Balfe Street.

The graduation was to be held in St Patrick's Chapel in Maynooth on 19th November 1987.

I met up with Father Jack in Dublin the week before.

'Marion, have you got a cap and gown?'

'Sister Anne said I can borrow one that she found in Ausilia. It's a bit crumpled but I'll make sure it is ironed.'

'Have you ever witnessed ceremonies in that chapel? The graduation will be on an even grander scale than St Patrick's Day celebrations. Cardinal O'Fiaich is presiding, you know.'

'So I've got to make sure of the gown?'

'If you're walking down the aisle with me I think I had better hire the outfit for you. Would you mind?'

After the ceremony in which we both received our diplomas in Religious Studies from the Pontifical University, Faculty of Theology, I persuaded a photographer who was touting for custom to follow the Cardinal

144

so that Father Jack and I could be taken alongside him.

As I left Maynooth on the bus into town to return to Baggot Street the next day, the seriousness of the decisions I was in the process of making frightened me. After the freedom and space I had been granted while studying during the past year, I was aware that I was now being forced to face up to how I was to live the rest of my life.

14

The Holy Veil

I sat up in bed and cut up my veil. The scissors weren't sharp and the thick fabric was slippery and hard to grip, but I kept cutting until the pieces scattered on my threadbare blanket in this Sisters of Mercy Convent, Baggot Street, Dublin, looked like black confetti.

Oh God, what have I done!

Dear Jesus, I'm so sorry! What's happening to me? I wanted to save the world from sin and hell but now I'm like an egg without a shell. I ache from head to toe. I get upset so easily and seem to be incapable of concentrating on anything. Is my breakdown back again?

Of course I couldn't breathe a word about my lack of faith to the other nuns. How could I tell them that I thought that they were wasting their lives? Yes, I had reached that point in my attitude to religious life. It was important to hide my disillusionment and uncertainty. I felt lonely, isolated, even a traitor. I had been in the Congregation of Salesian Sisters for twenty-eight years and at forty-three I wondered if I would be able to adapt to life outside the convent. I surmised that some of the others might well have battled with similar doubts and, having weighed up the pros and cons, concluded that it was easier to stay put.

Today, Jesus, I've arranged to meet Mona in town. She's probably lonely since she left the convent.

Mona had been a novice with me but had left. Like all the others who had gone, she had not been allowed to say goodbye or to tell anyone why she was going. I didn't know her that well but I had discovered recently she was settled near Dublin. I wondered how she was coping with regards to money and accommodation. I wanted to know if her family had come to her rescue. This was especially important to me because I was acutely aware of my family situation. However, I hoped that once I had fully recovered from the breakdown I had suffered before I went to Maynooth, I might be able to go back to teaching and so be able to support myself should I ever have to leave the Order.

★   ★   ★

I stretched to grab my towel from the back of the chair next to my iron bed. I mopped my clammy brow and hands. Very little air came through the skylight window in the narrow, creaky-floored bedroom I'd been allocated in this Dublin convent. The room was so small it was more like a cubicle. In fact, the nun sleeping next door to me said that this part of the convent had been a big dormitory used to house novices in the fifties and sixties when many more women wanted to become nuns.

I tried to shake the black bits of my veil through my sticky fingers. Perspiration seemed to be leaking from every pore and my heart was thumping like a washing machine on spin. I had cut up my veil. Most of the nuns in the convent where I was staying wore their veils at least when they went to Mass. Many of those in the Order still wore theirs all the time, especially back in England.

O Lord, this veil's been blessed so I can't just put the bits in the bin. No, they'll have to be burnt.

My plastic alarm-clock showed seven thirty. That's when nuns came out from Mass. I grabbed paper from my bin and the tin I used to keep my pencils in, pulled an old mack over my nightie, took the matches from the votive light in front of the statue of Our Lady and crept quickly down the rickety fire escape to the dustbins at the back of the convent. The latch was stiff and heavy but I managed to quietly prise the door open. The morning air cooled me. I hid behind the shed and tried to stuff the slippery material into the narrow tin. I broke a dry twig from a bush, poked and prodded and lit the paper. The fabric smouldered. I held it from me and as I blew on my scorched fingers I prayed:

Jesus Christ, please help me!

Sister Honoria came out to empty the water cruets on the roses. She didn't look in my direction. But strains of singing warned me that it was time to hide the evidence behind the bin and make for the fire escape. Shaking and looking back over my shoulder, I scampered up the stairs again and had to crouch down when I saw Sister Therese shuffling down the shiny parquet corridor inside.

I got back to my room and collapsed on my bed. As I lay there, for the umpteenth time I questioned why it was that I agreed to lodge with these Sisters of Mercy in a dark, grey stone convent with massive iron bars on the lower windows and a big, heavy front door. Only a few evenings before, when I was travelling past on the top of a bus, one of the students on the secretarial course with me said it looked like a prison. These were her remarks even though she'd never seen the pseudo oak panelling and the Silence notices on the faded green walls. Neither did she have to edge past the tramps pathetically begging round the entrance.

All the bell-ringing was so archaic. One bell sounded for one Sister, two for another and three short ones for Sister So and So. I couldn't imagine ordinary people, people that the nuns called 'lay', putting up with this. The laity were not allowed past the highly polished parlour where there was a big statue of their foundress, Mother Catherine McAuley. Even one of our nuns who was helping me with my luggage remarked on the number of pious magazines and booklets like *The Sacred Heart Messenger* and *The Novena* and the strategically placed collection boxes.

'You wouldn't need to have a delicate conscience, would you?' was what she said.

Another thing that was strange was that there were no homely smells coming from the kitchen. In fact it felt as though I was trapped in a funeral parlour or the antiseptic zone of a hospital.

But then, on the other hand, I was more than fed and found. I was often welcomed to watch *The Late, Late Show* with them. Besides, all I had to do was follow the timetable and turn up for prayers. I hoped that things might improve once I started my secretarial course. I was very fortunate to have been granted permission to experiment with a career change in the hope that my health would be restored. A big consequence of this was that, while I was on a course with 'ordinary people', I would not have to wear my habit.

However, experimenting with wearing ordinary clothes proved to be very daunting. Apart from my time in Maynooth when I had abandoned the veil, I had worn convent clothes from the age of fourteen so I had to sum up a lot of courage to brave it out in lay clothes, especially in the city. With the five pounds I'd been given for this purpose, I bought a beige skirt, creamy blouse and dark brown tweed jacket in Trócaire charity shop.

There were no mirrors in the convent, but then I had managed without any for years. Should we need to see our reflections we knew how to put a sheet of paper behind panels of glass on cupboards. I realised that the blouse was big and baggy and the elasticated waistband of the shirt hugged too tightly. But it was my hair that was the biggest problem. It had repeatedly been hacked and washed in anything from soda to washing powder. As I struggled to comb it under into the pageboy style that I had many years ago, there was the 'one two, one two' knock that signalled the arrival of Sister Mary D, the nun who slept and studied in the room next door.

'Come on in! What d'you think?' I asked as I did a twirl.

'You look fine,' she smiled.

'Only fine?' I joked.

'Well, you've still got a curler here at the back.'

'D'you know, going without my veil is what I'm dreading most. Hair that's been covered up for so long doesn't just spring back to life.'

I turned to face her, trailing my fingers through my limp tresses. She looked so small and burly, wrapped in her navy-blue habit.

'Marion, you're brave. You've done so much to sort things out for yourself. I couldn't do that. All those decisions: London to Dublin, out to Maynooth University and now this secretarial course. You're handling it all very well. 'Good on you!' is what I say. It takes a lot of courage. I admire you.'

I rubbed my hands together, sat down on the bed and smiled at her while thinking that, kind as she was, she would never replace Sister Maeve. Somehow Maeve and I still managed to confide in each other in spite of the fact that we had been warned about special relationships. We kept up our loving friendship but the spontaneity had gone out of our relationship. It was as if we were always on guard, against each other and ourselves, or at least that was the way I felt. Worse than having to guard against any physical demonstrations of affection was the silence we had to keep up about the fact we had been warned.

Dedicated Maeve had always been so sure of her calling. Remarkably, she was now still convinced that Jesus had chosen us to 'Save others while we saved ourselves'. She continued to teach a class of thirty-four of the most deprived Inner London seven to eight-year-olds. She faithfully followed the advice of our Mother General and in fact recently her letters had become preachy at the same time that I was questioning everything.

'Where have you gone, Marion?' Sister Mary D waved the comb in front of my face.

'Sorry! I'll brush my hair under one more time. Meeting this ex-nun Mona today is like doing undercover work. I want to find out if she has a job, where she lives, if she's lonely and lots of other things. Although we were together in the same community as novices we weren't friends, you know. All I want to know is what happens if one leaves this outfit!'

'Oh, so one is on one's way out, is one?' Sister Mary D retorted.

'Now, haven't I told you often enough that

I'm incapable of making decisions? Amn't I already taking a gigantic step going on this secretarial course?'

Over and over again I'd thought how much easier it was to stay put. After all, I'd been a nun for most of my life. In fact, I had been a nun for as long as Jesus lived on this planet.

'Well, there's no harm in finding out, investigating, as it were. Where're you meeting?'

'Usual place where folk seem to meet in Dublin, Mary — under Clerys' Clock in O'Connell Street. We're to meet at four and she's suggested we'll eat in the store restaurant.'

I counted myself fortunate in acquiring a good neighbour like Sister Mary D, in this big traditionally run convent. During the last few days I had told her a few facts about myself. She knew that I was a primary school teacher who earned my stripes in tough London schools and that I had a degree from London University and just graduated with a Pastoral Theology certificate from Maynooth University. She knew about my secretarial course. But there was a whole lot more I had no intention of telling her.

15

Under Clerys' Clock

While the priest was hearing the nuns' confessions, I crept down a dark corridor past the sacristy. The incense made me want to sneeze. Someone coughed. I hid behind a statue of Saint Joseph and spied the back of Sister Honoria as she shuffled into chapel. Breathless, I reached the back door. The sleeves of my baggy blouse were uncomfortably scrunched up in the sleeves of my tight cardigan. Fresh air blew through my hair and in and out of my limbs and I felt naked without my long enveloping habit. Embarrassed, I avoided people's looks by keeping my head down and walking quickly towards town.

My plans were to sit on a bench in Stephen's Green and eat the banana and roll I'd kept from supper the previous night. Then I would amble round the shops in Grafton Street and eventually cross the bridge spanning the River Liffey to arrive in O'Connell Street in time to meet Mona under Clerys' clock.

As I walked along I prayed:

Dear Jesus, will you punish me if don't keep my promises? I was among those of our nuns who said that we ought to return to our mission of living and working in the poorer areas of our big cities. I want to stay but . . . you know I'm not well. I should be celebrating my Silver Jubilee. What is your Holy Will for me?

'Escaped, have you? My two are off into the shops spending their money. Teenagers! Fine for them! Still, I'm not complaining. Hopefully they're an investment against the loneliness of old age. Are your lot in there too?

Jesus, what does this scrawly, shrieking woman who's plonked herself next to me mean?

I had been sitting quietly watching the ducks when this woman started talking to me about escaping. Then I remembered that I was not wearing my habit and so she would not have realised that I was a nun.

'Don't look so shocked! I do love them. In fact they're my pride and joy but they want so much! No use telling them that we didn't have all these gadgets and things, is it?'

I couldn't even attempt to answer her. I had been used to people smiling at me, opening doors and showing respect for my religious habit. I was incapable of coping with this familiarity. Somehow I managed to stand, force a smile and catch my tears on my lip as I moved off.

Lord Jesus, so this is what it will be like if I leave? And the children bit? I'm too old to have any of my own!

My blood boiled. I tore off my cardigan and wanted to strip off my stupid crumpled blouse.

As I marched out of the park and across the road I saw my scowling face in a mirror of the posh hairdresser's on the corner.

Everything is happening too quickly and there are too many people talking and laughing and going off in all directions.

I tried to mingle with the crowds in Grafton Street but found myself being pushed along. I wanted to stop and stare and take stock of how people dressed and behaved.

A Traveller woman called out: 'Four hot cross buns for a pound!'

I bought some, escaped into Brown Thomas department store and made my way to the restaurant.

I had been in that restaurant before and I knew that I had to find a table and wait until a waitress noticed me. I saw two older women about to leave a small table in the corner, so I firmed up my trembling legs and managed to walk straight over as soon as they moved off. I sat down quietly and took out my pen and notebook and pretended that I had something important to write.

A woman at the table in front of me draped the silk-lined jacket of her smart navy suit over her chair. Her cream blouse fitted her petite body beautifully. Her knee-length tailored skirt showed off her long slim legs. She had a matching leather bag and high-heeled shoes. Her gold earrings, necklace and bracelet were studded with sapphire stones. Her bigger-built friend was equally elegantly dressed in a beige trouser suit with a lime-green flouncy blouse and accessories and pearl jewellery. I eavesdropped on their conversation about the wedding they had been invited to. Coffee, croissants and perfume smells mingled together.

'Is madam ready to order?'

I wasn't up to being called 'madam'. I wanted my drink to last a long time so I ordered lemon tea and jug of hot water.

Oh God, I've managed it! I'm OK!

Then I handed her money and she gave me a quizzical look and told me that I would get the bill when I had finished. Hot springs gushed though me and I hoped that no one had witnessed my mistake. I was too frightened to look around and worried that I would not be able to carry through my plan of spending a long time there watering down my lemon tea and nibbling my hot cross bun when no one was looking. Sure enough, a few minutes later she came back to ask me if I'd like anything else and, when I said no, she handed me the bill. Then I made the biggest mistake of all. As I stood I reached to adjust my veil, realised I was not wearing one, and had to pretend that I was flicking back my hair.

Loving Jesus, please help me to walk across this restaurant! I feel like you when the crowds jeered you.

Everything felt wrong: my hair, my clothes, the jerky walk and sweaty body. Once again I long for the comfort of my habit and the respect that it merited.

Handling money was a big problem. I'd had none since I left home aged fourteen. We were obliged to ask permission for everything and, on the rare occasions we paid for a prescription or bought some underwear, we were given the amount it was expected to cost and were required to return with a receipt and the exact change and write a detailed account in an expenses book kept in a drawer for that purpose. Since our community begged at the market for most of our food and our clothes were either made or bought in bulk, I had no idea of the cost of anything. Therefore it was agreed that, while living in this other convent, I was to be given fifty pounds a month allowance in order to learn how to cope. Sometimes I would be only ten days into the month when I had already used up half of the money. Normally though, because all my meals were provided, I did not have to worry unduly. It was really only when I had to eat out that I had to be careful.

When wearing my habit I had never felt free to wander round a department store. When we were given permission to buy our own underwear, it was a big problem. Up until then knickers had been made by the linenarian and we did not wear bras. Most of our nuns still didn't go out to buy shop-made underwear. It was embarrassing standing in a lingerie department wearing a habit, especially if the assistant was someone you had taught.

I flashed back to when we'd started to wear coats instead of the traditional Italian-style shawl. A shop assistant in the Bentalls' department store, said, 'If you're searching for an anorak-type coat may I suggest you go to the market stalls?' Then she led me to the window overlooking Kingston Market and pointed out the stalls. I wanted to hit her and fall into her arms at the same time. But then, how was she to understand that I was feeling angry enough to want to punch her and so weak that I longed to be held, supported and embraced, simultaneously.

I arrived at our meeting place early enough to wander round Clerys' perfume counter. I saw women lifting the bottles and dabbing some on, so I thought I'd have a go. Then I caught sight of my pale face and protruding eyes in a mirror and panicked.

I have no lipstick on so everybody will know I am a nun.

I felt so sticky that I decided to wait in the doorway. I stood among the crowds who didn't queue like they do in England, but held back until the bus arrived and boarded together.

Only five minutes to go.

Lord, supposing she doesn't turn up? After all, there's nothing in it for her. Besides, even though we have been novices together we don't really know each other. What will she be wearing? Will I recognise her? She could take one look at the way I am dressed and scarper.

As the clock chimed three she stood in front of me dressed in bold shades of red. Sturdy, with crow-black hair drawn back from her determined facial features, she switched on a smile as she shoved her hand out to be shaken. She walked into the store saying, 'Follow me!' and I found myself being jolted in a queue in a bustling restaurant. Her clipped Newry accent matched her martial manner.

It was noisy. People of all ages were chattering. Round tables with dainty white cloths were barely separated from the clothes rails of the children's clothes department. A couple of young women had five brightly dressed youngsters between them, two in high chairs spilling food all round while the others picked and mixed burgers, chips and ice cream, at the same time as entwining their limbs round the silvery lightweight seating. An old woman, with an expensive-looking velvet jacket draped over her chair, seemed to be struggling to get her false teeth to go up and down into her cream bun at the same time as grinning and conversing with another woman.

Confronted by diverse smells and the loud din, I began to think it was all too much when Mona turned to me and snapped, 'It's Shrove Tuesday. I'm having the pancakes and pot of tea for £1.99 on special offer. I suggest you have the same.'

The man behind banged his tray into mine, but it didn't matter because I was so relieved that the choice had been made. The distance between the trays and the till seemed too short given all the information that had to be read and all the decisions that had to be taken into consideration. Without Mona's direction I would have had to gauge what I needed to eat and drink, see how much it cost and have my money ready to pay at the same time as manipulating a tray along a rack beneath the counter. But, even though I copied Mona, I did not manage to have my money out when I arrived at the cashier and she paid. I felt my face redden. Should I offer her the money? What did people do?

I was about to make for a quiet corner of the restaurant when she plonked her tray down in the middle of the crowd and said, 'What's it like in the Baggot Street convent?'

'M-mona,' I stammered and wanted to add, 'Keep your voice down.'

She sat and continued: 'Why you agreed to get mixed up with that ancient lot is beyond me! All that bowing and scraping!' She put a forkful of pancake in her mouth.

'It's nice in here,' I said, hoping to get her off the subject.

'Sure, isn't there enough guilt and sin in the Church without adding to it?'

I managed to come out with, 'Mona, everyone will hear you.'

'And what harm if they do? Besides, nobody's in the slightest bit interested anyway.'

As Mona squeezed lemon over her pancake, I looked at the love-struck couple that only had eyes for each other at the nearby table. She was right; nobody was listening.

'They will only start to be curious if you whisper, so why don't you eat up while your pancake is still warm?'

A long period of quiet ensued while I struggled to swallow the bits of pancake sticking in my throat and she looked at her watch and around at everyone else and said nothing. Eventually, pushing my plate away, I tried to smile.

'When I agreed to stay with these nuns, I didn't realise what it would be really like. But I had to stay somewhere convenient while I followed the course I've chosen.' I emphasised 'chosen'.

She looked through me and said nothing.

I continued, 'I would have preferred to live in a rented room, but I was asked to compromise and agreed to rent a study bedroom with these nuns. So that's how I've ended up on the third floor of their old convent.' My voice was whining.

She continued looking beyond me and raised her eyebrows.

I forced a laugh and said, 'All kinds of bell-ringing goes on, you know, and shuffling about in the semi-dark after the recitation of Compline. During the Great Silence water bottles are filled and hot chocolate is made and camomile tea is brewed.'

For a brief moment Mona's eyes met mine.

So I went on: 'These nuns pray even more than we do and they give a great deal of respect to the clergy. And the older nuns still wear bonnets and long habits. But I've noticed some of the younger ones are a bit rebellious. And they've all received permission to wear a little clip brooch instead of those big crucifixes they used to wear.'

Mona glared at me. I felt awkward and strained. There were fewer people in the restaurant now so it was much quieter. Nothing was said. What was I to do?

Eventually I said, 'I missed Mass this morning.' She didn't react so I added, 'I cut up my veil.'

Mona focused a sharp look at me as she said, 'So maybe you do want to leave the convent?' Then she stood up and shoved her chair under the table as she added, 'In or out, it is your decision and you have to live with the consequences.' With that she shook my hand and walked away through the store and was gone.

I felt very lonely and confused as I waited in O'Connell Street for the bus to take me back to the convent. The bells tolled for the Angelus prayer and two nuns dressed in long flowing habits came round the corner from the Pro-Cathedral and made the sign of the cross over themselves, while in the queue right in front of me a young couple petted and kissed each other. I began to fantasise to take away the gnawing loneliness.

16

Weighing Up

Dear Jesus, I'll ask the nuns where I'm staying if I can use their phone. Calling England will cost a lot though and my superiors will receive the bill and I'll be quizzed. It's half past six. What'll Maeve be doing now? If they've still got the same timetable in Battersea she'll be having supper with the community. They'll be sitting at table while the life of some saint or other is being read aloud. So when the phone rings whoever's turn it is will go and find out who's calling whom. Then everybody'll know my business because she'll have to go back and whisper to the Superior and ask if Sister Maeve can have permission to take the call. Poor Maeve is still caught in all this rigmarole! Kind, caring Maeve loves you so much, Jesus. Maybe she's the one who is doing the right thing in staying in the convent? I have to talk to her tonight! Blow the lot of them! I'll just have to find a way. What if I pretend I'm someone else?

From the top of the bus I could see

canoodling couples and folk all dressed up making for restaurants and pubs.

'Well, I never! If it isn't yourself! And where might you be going?'

It was 'the bold Peggy' as we used to call her when we were on the Pastoral Course in Maynooth and there was laughter in her voice. She was bending over me, her face close to mine. No habit; casual as you like in a turquoise suit and off-white blouse. Black patent, matching bag and high heels, lipstick, the lot. No-one would suspect *her* of being a nun.

'Well, am I glad to see you!' I cried. 'And where are you off to yourself?'

There was devilment in her eyes. 'Come on!' she said as she yanked me up off my seat and pushed me down the bus in front of her.

Once on the pavement she held me at arm's length, saying, 'Marion, you look great. I hardly recognised you at first without the habit. Now, I'm meeting a friend for a meal and you're more than welcome to join us and there's no need to worry, it'll be *my* treat.'

'I'd love to chat, but I've just eaten and I'm trying to prepare myself for the 'one square meal' permitted tomorrow on Ash Wednesday.'

'Wouldn't you forget all those restrictions and come up and be sociable and partake of whatever you feel able to enjoy. Come on?' she coaxed. 'Aren't you supposed to be having the year out to decide on your future? Don't tell me that it's the Will of God that you live in misery!'

While we supped our beverages in a cosy nook of the restaurant I told Peggy about my unsuccessful meeting with Mona. I heard myself saying, 'I don't know what to do for the best, Peggy. I really enjoyed the year with ye all in Maynooth. The five of us doing the Pastoral Theology course had great craic together, but now I feel so lonely and I'm wondering if I'm making a big mistake in leaving.'

She screwed up her forehead and, pressing back her fingers one at a time, she quizzed, 'I've asked you this before but I'll put these questions to you again. Do you honestly think you'll be happy going back to teach or even do parish work in England? Do you really believe that the kind of religious life lived by your friend Maeve would satisfy you now?' She pointed her finger at me. 'Answer me straight now, Marion!'

'I like Maeve a lot and she's changed job and seems to be doing so much good and she's so convinced and upright ... ' I struggled.

'That's it, Marion. She's *convinced*. Cop

yourself on, can't you? No, I take that back. That's unfair. You're in the middle of deciding. No, why don't you keep an open mind and do this secretarial course and see what happens. Surely to God you'll know one way or another by the time you've finished?'

I warmed my hands round the mug of hot chocolate and didn't answer.

She leaned over, put her arms around me and said, 'These are difficult times, I know, for all of us.'

'Yes. We had so many meetings. I suppose they did their best to involve us at the grass roots, you know. But the orders come from Rome. The Italians seem to be good at telling others what to do while remaining experts at getting round regulations themselves.'

'There were so many changes in such a short space of time, weren't there?'

'That's what shook my trust. I mean, things that we had been told would go on forever suddenly didn't matter any more! Take the habit for example . . . '

As I was recounting this to Peggy, a priest I recognised from one of the hostels in Maynooth came into the restaurant and slipped in and seated himself beside her.

She turned and said, 'Well, as you know each other there's no need for me to introduce ye.' He gave her a peck on the cheek and leaned over to shake hands with me.

'We just bumped into each other and I'm off home now,' I said as I leapt up to go.

'That's the quickest put-down I've had for a long time,' responded Seán.

'There's no need to worry about shocking Seán. He and I talk about all sorts. Why d'you think we meet up in here away from it all?'

'But I'll have to get back to the convent before it's too late!'

'Relax, will you? You have plenty time yet! And Seán's got a car. In fact, you can come back with me for tonight. You know there're plenty of beds in our place.'

So, before I knew it, we all had food in front of us and we continued our chatting.

'You won't believe this, Seán,' I said, 'but our Novice Mistress — '

'*Mistress!* Well, what am I to make of that?' said he with raised eyebrows.

'Being as it is an Italian outfit we actually had to call her '*Signora Maestra*'. Anyways, 'She Who Trained Us Before We Made Our Vows' had all the private parts of the cherubs on the ceiling of our study painted with a veiling effect.' Encouraged by their laughter I continued, 'She once had a whole batch of Jelly Babies melted down to stop us seeing their naked bodies!'

They howled with laughter, hands over mouths, and rocking back in their chairs.

'Is it any wonder we felt so guilty?' asked Seán.

'Sex and even the act of procreation were associated with sin. My own ma told me,' said Peggy in a Dublin accent, 'that after my brother was born she was not allowed to receive Holy Communion until after she'd been 'churched'. The way she used to tell it was: *'There was the priest looking down on me, and he in his white, frilly, cotton shirt. I being made to feel dirty and sinful in a big dark church and he smirking and not having a clue what giving birth was all about!'* Isn't it a man's world?'

Peggy and I pointed at Seán and we all laughed again.

'There seems to have been an obsession with purity and chastity. Where did that come from?' mused Seán.

'It's in our Rule book,' said Peggy, 'that we each received the *gift* of chastity. Well, I must have been out when that was doled out!'

Seán winked at Peggy.

So it was that we recounted memories and roused emotions for an hour or two that night. I told Seán that we were expected to be able to change our clothes anywhere, even in the middle of a market place, without showing any part of our body, simply by using certain manoeuvres.

Peggy then admitted that on Thursday afternoon, when the novices were allocated partners before being sent out for a walk, she worked out that by standing at the opposite side of the room from her friend there was many a time when they succeeded in being with each other. That was in spite of the hang-ups about novices forming particular friendships.

It took me a long time to get to sleep in a strange bed in Maynooth that night.

I must talk to Maeve tomorrow. We've stuck it out for so long through thick and thin, I told myself as I fell asleep.

17

Looser Living

'*Dia duit!* Peggy at your service! Would madam like cereal, tea or coffee?'

I grunted as I tried to squeeze my eyes open.

'Sorry. It's a grand day and I thought we could get a head start and go out on our bikes. I'm making sandwiches, so what d'you think?'

I pushed the top half of me up onto my elbow. 'Great. I'm coming down.'

'No, stay Marion, it's breakfast in bed. Would a bowl of porridge do? I've some on.'

'That would be lovely.'

Looking round, I prayed.

Dear Jesus, thank you for bringing me here. Amn't I lucky us nuns have got this lackadaisical set-up? That's the beauty of this hostel! I was so lonely at the bus stop last night that I had to resort to my secret painkiller again! Remembering any time that I had been hugged or romantic scenes from my historical novels! Recalling them so vividly that it took away the gnawing pain of feeling lonely. I hope this imagining does not offend you . . . but what else can I do?'

A phone. But it would cost so much. Wouldn't it be great if Maeve answered?

Even if I had the courage to ring it dawned on me that our Battersea nuns would probably still be in chapel. So I showered, dressed in borrowed shorts, and in no time we were zooming round the lanes of Kilcock, the air rushing through my hair and my goose-pimply legs getting used to exposure.

I felt my lips quivering into a smile as I imagined hearing the nostalgic voice of HV Morton in his book *In Search of Ireland*. I had read this in preparation for my return to the homeland. The bits I loved were where he describes '*the brown-green Wicklow Hills clear cut against the sky*' and how '*there is laughter in the cadence of the Irish voice*' and the promise that '*it is impossible to be lonely there because the art of talking is a game with no rules often referred to as 'codology'.*' All this was real now. My feet gripped the bicycle pedals more firmly when I recalled how Morton refers to The Easter Rising that took place in the GPO in O'Connell Street. I blinked through proud tears as I remembered my mother telling me that my great-uncle Michael Colivet took part in The Rising and became Minister for

Finance in the first Dáil Eireann.

Not a word passed between Peggy and me as we eased our way down boreens edged with so many shades of green, splashed with fuchsia and blossoming white hawthorn bushes, encompassing the lush fields of Kildare's stud farms.

After some time Peggy pulled in off the road and I came up beside her.

'How about here? There's a stream over there and we've ready-made tables in the rocks.'

'Grand. What could be better?'

'I'm ravenous,' said Peggy, propping her bike against a shady tree and reaching into her wicker basket for eats. Tall as she was she looked plumpish in shorts. Her long white spindly legs showed broken veins but her top covered her busty upper half.

We munched our rolls and cupped clear spring water to slake our thirst. Wrens, crows and a pair of pheasant didn't seem to mind us sharing their playground. Birds I couldn't name swooped, dipped and sang.

'I still can't believe my luck in being allowed to do that pastoral course here in Maynooth last year.' Peggy smiled between bites, so I went on, 'But I have to do such a lot of thinking and deciding now. So much soul-searching. Our nuns here in Ireland seem so liberated. You're encouraged to think for yourselves. I was so angry and broken when I landed but now . . . well, I couldn't pick a fight even if I wanted, with any of ye . . . I'm accepted as I am . . . '

Peggy unzipped her banana and nodded, got up, threw me a huge smile and shook her crumbs off before saying, 'I'm off for a wander.'

I tidied my things away and sat on a flatter rock and allowed my addled mind to amble back and forth, pondering, searching, weighing the consequences, realising that things had already begun to change for me.

'Have you fallen asleep?' It was Peggy back from her wander. 'Yes, you really did enjoy the course — especially the extra-curricular activities! You enjoyed that guitar singing. And we all knew when you felt a sudden rush of hormones because you'd play 'You Fill Up My Senses' on your recorder!'

I smiled. She winked. I flung a pebble in the stream.

'Usen't we have great craic?' I said. 'Sure didn't two of the lads in the Salesian hostel fall in love with students and leave . . . and what about that fellow, forty years a priest, going off with that nun who used to go to him for spiritual advice?'

'Things were really hotting up then,

weren't they?' said Peggy. She put her hand over her mouth and rocked with laughter as she screamed out, 'D'you remember how you got so fed up watching those blessed bishops parading round St Joseph's Square, all dressed up in flowing black robes with pink trimmings that you went out and bought bright pink wool and knitted yourself a bright pink tubular headpiece with matching cuffs and joined their fashion show. You're a howl, d'you know that?'

'Am I? But I'm still pretty scared that I'm doing the wrong thing in leaving.'

'But you cut up your veil? And you told your Sister Superior that you needed more time to think and you've managed to get yourself on a secretarial course. What's making you do all that?'

'Peggy, I don't know. All I do know is that I feel sick inside. When I think of when I was in Bermondsey and all I wanted to do was to lie on the road and let a red double-decker mow me down and — ' My body began to shake and storm-sized tears flooded from my eyes.

Peggy moved to put her arm behind my back to support me.

'It's just I can't make sense of it all. I mean 'twas Maeve that encouraged me to talk to Sister Superior and they were both very good to me. I keep hearing Sister Superior's words,

'I want you to be happy and I'll do all in my power to help. I'm happy giving my life to Christ — maybe you can do this in a different way.''

Peggy whispered in a laughing voice, 'I can see you in Sister Margaret's room last May, seated cross-legged on the floor, leaning against her bed and telling jokes. You weren't frightened then, far from it!'

I straightened up and Peggy dropped her arm and I went on remembering as we cycled back to Maynooth.

18

So Much for Chastity

I had never really looked at my body and so was delighted when another student on the secretarial course told me that it stuck out in all the right places.

Here we go again! I'm on fire with sexual urges and I don't know what to do with myself! Please God, forgive me but I feel like battering down the convent doors and racing starkers all the way to the pub on the edge of Stephen's Green and dancing to the beat of fiddle music!

I longed to dance and sing the night away at a Gaelic gig. Instead, there I was leaning against an old brown wooden bench in a depressing dim laundry room on the third floor of the drab Baggot Street convent, taking my turn to use the washing machine. The nuns were watching the *News at Nine* to determine which world disaster zone to pray for when they recited the Divine Office. The Great Silence began at ten and they would retire with their cocoa and spiritual reading books. I had barely an hour to get my load in so as not to disturb them when it reached the spin programme.

'And what, may I ask, might a young slip of a girl be doing inside these concrete walls so early in the night?' Úna said as she pushed the door open. She was a lay student following a course while lodging in Baggot Street convent.

'Rapunzel, Rapunzel, let your hair down so that your prince can climb up this tower!' I teased.

'Once I have finished my last exam this Friday, I tell you, I'll be flying out of here with gusto-oh! Oh! Oh! There'll be no holding me back. Sure, it's a good place to keep distractions out, but as for living? Well, you might as well be entombed in here.'

'God, don't talk to me about it.' I found myself taking the Lord's name in vain. 'Can't you see my hormones racing up and down my body, bursting and breaking out from every orifice? Look out! Take shelter!'

'Aren't you delighted you're still a woman through and through after all those years of abstention, Marion? Why don't you put your wash in and come along to my place. I've the linen cupboard separating me from the old nun on the other side and besides I've been told she's hard of hearing.'

'But don't you have to study for the next exam?'

' 'Tis celebrating I am tonight. I've sweated more than blood today with a three-hour Social Philosophy paper. No, as Saint Benedict of old recommends, 'Moderation in all things', and besides not another thing will go in my brain this night. Come on, girl, I have a bottle so let's get liberated. The washing'll go through its motions by itself. Come on!'

Forty-six-year-old Úna, mother of grown twins and happily married to Brendan, had decided to accept a grant to update herself in lecturing at Limerick University by gaining a Pastoral Diploma at a nearby centre for religious studies. She had opted for the convent accommodation simply because she was only required to pay for the five nights she used the room. On Friday night she caught the cheap student bus back down the country to her home in the prosperous South Circular Road area of the Limerick metropolis.

Tall and athletic, Úna sported chocolate-brown jogging pants and a cream cotton top. It was obvious from the lighter roots round her sharp-featured face that her mousy brown hair had been touched up. I followed her darting greeny-brown eyes round her tiny

182

spartan study. The white-painted single iron bed reminded me of the type I had slept in for aeons. A matching locker and bookshelf were the only furniture she had. Her clothes were in a cover bag on a hook at the back of her door. There were no perfumed scents competing with sterile convent smells there.

'Welcome to my cell!' she laughed. 'Here, sit on my bed. Sorry about the lack of an armchair. Dream on — no such luxuries, I'm afraid. You'd think I'd joined up, wouldn't you? Of course my hubby hasn't seen the ensuite, it being within the enclosure. You know, by rights I should be one of the nuns to be allowed up here, so what chance would there be of a man getting in? Now there's a thought. Just as well hubby can't see where I live 'cause he would never have agreed to this poverty.' She poured me a plastic beaker full of red wine.

'Is it strong?' I pointed to the drink.

'It's poteen,' she said seriously, then laughed. 'Go on now with you! Roches Stores 'On Offer' plonk. It's not bad for what it is. It'll do you no harm and in fact it might dampen down your raging passions. But maybe you don't want to stop them erupting?'

Una plied me with questions about what had been bringing me to decide I wanted to leave the convent and I heard myself replying with such vehemence that it became clear how angry I was about missing out on what were most likely the best years of my life.

'I suppose you'll be rushing out now to find the man of your dreams?' she probed.

Instantly I wished I hadn't told her so much about myself. That was definitely something I would have to learn. She was not my Sister Superior and so I did not have to give her an account of all I was doing. Still, I needed to talk that night and the wine helped.

I told her how for years the only men I had seen were priests dressed in layers of long flowing Mass vestments or full-length black soutanes. But as our conversation went on, I discovered she was disconcertingly conservative. She didn't find it amusing when I told her that some of us had christened our local bishop 'No Physical Contact' because he didn't approve of us shaking hands at the Sign of Peace ceremony during Mass and he certainly did not want to witness any of his congregations getting even more intimate and hugging or, God forbid, kissing each other. While she agreed that the Church needed the modernisation that came after the Second Vatican Council, she was apprehensive that too much change could lead to the downfall of high moral standards.

'Don't get me wrong, Marion, but we have to control our bodies otherwise sexual urges will take over. Even priests are not immune from these strong feelings. All this sloppy, airy-fairy, clappy-happy liturgy lacks theological foundation. You can correct me if I'm speaking out of turn, but maybe you wouldn't be looking to break your vows if you had met some of the learned Jesuits we have lecturing to us. Sorry now, I hope I'm not upsetting you but I have to speak my mind.'

Forgive me, God, but what an insensitive bitch! So that was why she invited me in! Has she taken it upon herself to save my soul?

I had to get away. 'Sorry, that's the spinner stopped. Must go.'

I pulled open her door and left.

Sick, blinded with tears, shaking with anger, I tugged my clothes out of the machine, ran back to my room, bolted my door, flung myself down on my bed and sobbed. I was glad I was in darkness when Úna banged at my door. The wine eventually got me to sleep but I had a massive nightmare not unlike that described in Dante's *Inferno*. I was dragged down into dark tunnels of hell and was punished in mind and body for all my sins of impurity in thought, word and deed. I felt so guilty for all those times I had indulged in reading descriptions of passion from Anya Seton's historical novels. That was when I had taken the fly cover from the meditation book to hide *Katherine* so I could take it into chapel in order to arouse my passions and so cope with my longings and utter loneliness. I deserved to burn and suffer in the flames for all eternity. I woke up screaming and found myself sitting upright in the middle of the night. Angry again, I felt I hated the likes of Úna. Foolish me for thinking that because we both hailed from Limerick we could have much in common. I resolved I'd keep far away from her from then on.

The only way I could get myself back to sleep that night was by reliving once more the wonderful sensations I had experienced in Father Mike's arms, imagining the smell of his tweedy jacket and the beating of his heart.

I woke up lonesome and exhausted in my single bed between cheap, faded pink polyester sheets the next morning. It was still a little dark, but the seven o'clock bell had gone to remind those who had slept in that the priest would be saying Mass soon. I couldn't go. I would have to keep out of Úna's way. So I would have to miss breakfast too. I wouldn't be able to get out of the convent either until the main door had been unlocked. Pity now that I hadn't sneaked a roll and a banana from the table after supper. So I got dressed and timed my going downstairs to coincide with the priests going onto the altar and escaped through the sacristy door.

Dear Jesus, I'm off down to Stephen's Green to ponder on why I was not given the gift of chastity!

It was early autumn and when I reached the centre of the park I sat on a damp bench on the outer rim of the stone circle that edges the concrete monument in the middle of this oasis of calm. Warm hues from a palette of vibrant amber to mottled chestnut foliage protected the lingering roses. Part of me wanted to answer the call of the Mass bells pealing from University Chapel, but the stumbling, weaker self wanted to hibernate and camouflage in the undergrowth to recover from my disturbed state of mind.

According to the Rule Book of the Order, each person who had been accepted had proved, by treating her body hard and making it obey her, that she had been given this precious gift of chastity from God. She had accepted it in faith and in return offered up her '*powers of loving*'. It stated too, that this '*renders us like angels*' and '*All good things come to those who, even in this mortal life, possess this inestimable treasure'.*

Lord, God, have I been given this treasure? Why else, for the last twenty-five years of my life, have I been raging with sexual cravings and yet denying my body any physical pleasure? I puzzled too why, when I had voiced my concerns about this to my superiors, they had not appeared to be surprised. Did they too have these feelings? Were we all struggling to maintain an impossible lifestyle? Why did the priests I discussed this with become so embarrassed? Why was Mary Immaculate and the purity of mind, thought and deed of saints like Saint Dominic Savio put forward as models?

Dear Jesus, why did you create our bodies with bits and pieces we are not permitted to look at, never mind to make use of? I'm so muddled! Of course I know chastity and restraint are necessary and we can't go round lustful and irresponsible but . . .

I was bumped back into my senses by slick, early workers taking a short cut around by the lake. I made my way down Grafton Street and bought four bars of chocolate for a pound from a Traveller woman and walked past the footmen of the Westbury Hotel, catching the tempting whiff of ground coffee. Up in the luxurious ladies' toilets I gobbled something sweet to sustain me.

I took ages washing my hands with the perfumed soap and wiping them in paper towels that had much more substance than my bath towel. It seemed to be a complete waste to throw them away in the lovely brown pedal-dustbin after only one use.

As I looked at my fragile image reflected in the ornate frame of the mirror, I longed for Father Mike to hug me and take away my loneliness and pain. But he was miles away back in England, probably assuring some other nun that she could show Jesus just how much she loved him by hugging him tightly.

19

Getting Out

No doubt those in the know were saying, 'Spot the nun!'

I'd spent ages in the ladies' of The Westbury Hotel trying to put lipstick on and making sure that my slip wasn't showing. Each time I tried to sneak past the uniformed fellow on the door he'd eye me up and down. In the end I explained that I was nervous about starting a course at the Language, Secretarial and Business Centre, next door.

'Ah sure, there's nothing to concern yourself about. Every October 'tis the same. Young slips of girls so timid that their fathers have to accompany them creep through those doors, only to barge out into Grafton Street in June as if they own it!' He placed a reassuring hand on my shoulder before adding, 'But, if you don't mind me saying so, you look like a sensible woman.'

He winked and I made for the door and slunk in under the notice *Language, Secretarial and Business Centre.*

'You'll be Miss Dante. Am I right?' was

how the secretary in the low-cut blouse checked me in.

Miss! Miss! Dear God, I've lost myself already. I'm not one of those young flimsy things, but neither am I a teacher. There's no one my age here. Who do I side with? I've made a terrible mistake. Maybe, though, if I succeed in nothing else, I can help these youngsters.

A blonde gesticulating woman clapped her hands. Her stilettos raised her above us.

'Now, no matter what choices you've made, you'll each need an up-to-date CV. So will anyone who hasn't produced one please follow Gerry into that room.' She pointed and half a dozen followed, including me.

Ah, Jesus, what am I to do now? I don't want to give the game away! How'll I compose a CV without revealing my identity? Do I really have to do this?

'Don't look so bewildered. This will be an easy way to find your way into the group.'

I felt talons digging into my waist. No one had touched me there before. I smelt the teacher's tangy perfume before turning to glimpse tawny eyes.

Dear Jesus, how much does she know about me?

There was no back of the class. The six computers in the middle of the room were taken by giggling girls who seemed well acquainted.

O Lord, where do I go? If I'm to reveal my private stuff I don't want to be close to anyone, yet I don't know how to work one of these things!

'Marion. It is Marion, isn't it? Maybe you'd like to come up here next to Ciara?'

Ciara tossed back her wispy hair, winced a smile and whisked out the chair for me.

We listened and made notes up 'til coffee time.

God our Father, what now? They're all so young and frilly without a care in the world! What'll I talk about? Ciara has skipped away to her friend. They're shrieking and plotting.

When I joined the queue for the toilets a softly spoken girl behind me whispered, 'I owe it to my dad to pass this course.'

Her friend replied, 'My mother says it's worth every penny if I get a chance of working in Switzerland. A tax-free year there and I'll be well away. Then hopefully I'll be able to pay my parents back and get myself started.'

I turned and held out a hand. 'My name's Marion. I bet ye're already familiar with those computers?'

That's as far as I got with any of these ambitious, finishing-school girls.

From then on, every day I used the

Westbury's loos, ate one of the chocolate bars I bought cheaply from the Traveller women and ventured as far as Stephen's Green to eat a roll and banana or cheese during the lunch break.

Some days I'd walk past the Bank of Ireland in order to view the mysterious cashpoints. Some of the nuns at the convent said that when you used one you were in danger of someone brushing up against you and chalking a cross on your back so that they could rob you out of sight of the bank. This bank had a machine inside, but there was always a queue and I knew I'd need to spend ages examining it. One day I deliberately stood a short distance away from a woman and tried to watch what she did. I couldn't see properly so I moved nearer.

She jerked her head round and shouted: 'What in the Name of God do you think you're doing? Are you a complete eejit or what?' But when she saw my tears she finished off her business, came over and said, 'Well, if you were out to steal from me you'd have been long gone. So might I suggest you go over there and ask for help?' She nodded her curls towards the Customer Service counter. 'Because what you're doing out here could be construed as invading people's privacy.'

I gulped my 'Sorry!' and the following day

asked for someone to come out and help me. Fair dues, a big-glasses woman told me to come back when they were not so busy. So the day after that she patiently took me through the process, warning me that on no account was I to keep my pin number anywhere near my card.

* * *

Even though I got my clothes free from what was handed in to the convent or at very little cost in charity shops, I loved window-shopping in Grafton Street. I had discovered a shop that would buy designer-labelled clothes, so often I'd root through those handed in to the convent and sell to this place. We were free to avail ourselves of these clothes and sell them if we needed money to buy some other necessity.

After a few weeks I realised that I could try on clothes that I could not afford. This was great. I'd walk into Brown Thomas, take beautifully tailored clothes off the peg, go into the changing rooms and dream on.

Once when I was trying on a fitted blouse the assistant remarked, 'Aren't you the lucky one with the slim figure?'

That's when I realised that I was inclined to cover myself with loose and baggy clothes.

So when I saw a notice outside an exclusive retailers 'Fire Damaged Clothes at Reduced Prices' I bought my first pair of olive figure-hugging trousers.

★ ★ ★

'Will you be coming for the Retreat?' enquired Sister Agnes in Maynooth.

'Who's guiding it?'

'The lightning streak. Him with the guitar.'

'Oh don't! It's gentle Hugh, isn't it? My knees tremble and I go all . . .'

'So I'll count you in!' she giggled.

Hugh sang the hymn he had composed about John Bosco:

'Here is a man who found a way to make
The stars above our heads seem brighter
than the day!
He offered hope, he made a family of the
young,
By living freely, spending night and day
giving life away,
Finding hearts ready to respond

Chorus:
And so we keep this memory of his life,
Memory filled with joy and goodness,
Reaching out to everyone,

195

Calling us to love,
Bringing us to God with a message for
the world.'

'Gee, that's mighty! What an alluring air and such fitting words! An altogether captivating song-cum-hymn! That Hugh O'Donnell's a pure genius!'

'He's somehow managed to sum up the life of Don Bosco in three verses. Do you know, it's brought tears to my eyes!'

'What is it with Hugh and Saint John Bosco? He seems so content in his vocation.'

When Mass had ended and they'd all gone for coffee, Niamh, one of the five Salesian Sisters who did the Maynooth course with me, signalled me over to sit closer to her on the hard chapel bench.

'Well,' she said, sotto voce, 'that's it. I've been going round to that hunk John Dowling for counselling and he's managed to convince me that those of us who are frightened of the real thing go after the unattainable.'

'Wooah! Slow down now, will you? All that seems highfalutin to the likes of me!'

Niamh said, 'OK, well, the likes of you and me who have been inside since our youth have stifled our inclinations to love and be loved for so long that we're really scared of the real thing.'

'So we go for saints and priests who are very happy being priests, safe in the knowledge that there'll be no relationship involved? That actually makes a lot of sense and in fact explains why out in the real world we're not so brave . . . '

'So that's your experience?' asked Niamh.

'Well, when I'm in Dublin I shy away from making myself look attractive and I know I'd run a mile should anyone make a pass at me. Not that they would, mind you, if you saw what I wear.'

'Precisely. That's it. We're safe chasing the impossible.'

'But, d'you know, Niamh, my heart still thumps for St John Bosco. It was he who enticed me away from home all those years ago and I still think helping vulnerable youngsters the way he did can be so satisfying. Then on the other hand how am I going to cope with my boisterous hormones?'

'How indeed!' Niamh sighed. 'Well, come on in to join the others!'

As she held out her hand to haul me out to join the crowd, I noticed she was sporting nail varnish. Then I remembered that she always used to play 'Some Say Love' from *The Rose* on her guitar before she set off for her counselling.

20

Back to England

It was August 1988 and I was still struggling to learn how to swim against the tide of my life. Much like the Shannon that rises high up in County Cavan, from the time I had taken my vows, for twenty-five years I had been carried along from source to open sea. True that over the years my limpid beginnings had become stronger and more resourceful as I carved out a riverbed for myself, removing obstacles and surmounting hurdles en route. Again, like this great river, whose powers were successfully harnessed at Ardnacrusha to generate electricity for Limerick and its surrounds, my strength and energy had been galvanised into the saving of souls from sin, but I was left feeling exhausted and disillusioned when I reached the estuary plains.

Dear God, my Father, 'make up your mind time' has arrived again and caught me unprepared. My secretarial course is finished but what now? I don't want to return to our Streatham convent so why have the Sister

Superiors of England and Ireland gone ahead and booked my ticket without consulting me? But then maybe they had to do something because I'm incapable of knowing what I should do. I suppose I can't keep extending my exclaustration. Exclaustration! What a funny name they've given to this decision time!

⋆ ⋆ ⋆

'We are off into town tomorrow and more to the point, we've got the use of the car. You'd be very welcome to join us, Marion!'

I was visiting the nuns in Maynooth, craving their company because when I was in Baggot Street or out in the city I was always alone and lonely.

'Just the thing! I'd love a last look at the capital before I leave. Thanks, I'll take you up on that. When will ye be leaving?'

Dear Jesus, what is this Maynooth community up to? I bet they're trying to get me out of the way to spring some treat on me. They're so good to me. I've never been loved like this before. Aren't they a credit to old Ireland and amn't I so lucky?

Sure enough a great day in Dublin was had by all and that night when we returned the haunting tune of 'The Fields of Athenry' drew us down to the community room where there was a big notice attached to the curtains saying, '*Slán agus beannacht, Marion!*'. By that time I had enough Irish to know that translated into 'Goodbye and God bless you'.

I was clapped in by seven nuns snugly seated in armchairs arranged round two long coffee tables on which there was cutlery rolled up in orange serviettes and bowls of fruit, nuts, sweets and various nibbles.

There was a trolley laden with a selection of pizzas, quiches, cold meats and salad. And to drink: tea, coffee, Bailey's Cream and wine.

'Gosh! I . . . '

Sister Agnes put her hand under my arm and ushered me in. 'Come on now, up here to your seat of honour. I know you deserted us last year by staying with those Mercy nuns in Baggot Street while you did your course but you surely didn't think we'd leave you off back to England without a proper farewell, did you?'

We ate, sang, reminisced and moved the chairs back to dance. I was given a silver Claddagh ring of friendship. There were hugs and fond wishes nearer to midnight and I couldn't remember ever being made such a fuss of. The following day two cars of sad-looking Sisters and my priest friend,

Father Jack, came to the airport to wave me off.

★ ★ ★

No one met me at Gatwick. I hauled my case from trolley to train across London to Clapham Junction, trying to work out how I was going to manage to get it on a bus. It was a hot August day. The perspiration was streaming off me because I was wearing a thick Aran cardigan that I was unable to squeeze into the case. The wheels seemed to have a mind of their own and besides did nothing towards making it any easier to lift the case from train to the platform. Busy commuters opened the carriage doors before the train stopped. A young mother in a sari carrying a baby in one arm tried to pick up her folded pushchair with the other and get off. A grey-haired man extended his hands in order to hold back the two business chaps behind him from pushing all before them through the doors. I was standing behind these, desperate to reach my case next to the door and somehow get off before the bleep-bleep signals stopped pipping, the doors closed and the train moved on.

Panicking I shouted out, 'Please can someone hold the door? I want to get off!'

'All right. All right!'

The helping grey-haired man, waved his hand up and down in a slow-down-your-pace gesture, at the same time as a couple prodding me forward said, 'You're not the only one! Just keep your hand on the button, sir, and we'll all be all right.'

The crowd propelled my case off on to the platform. I sat on it until the guard waved the train on and, as he was making his way back to the security of his office, I waved and whined, 'Please would you give me a hand down the steps with my case?'

Fortunately, before he had time to respond, a low-sized old man in an anorak grasped the handle of the case and at great speed walked down the steps in front of me.

I ran after him repeating 'Thank you very much! Thank you!'

He beamed a toothy smile, dropped the case, turned round and went straight back up to the platform.

I continued out on to the main street. I knew I'd have to drag the case down to the crossing to catch the bus travelling towards Streatham from the other side of the street. Once I got to the bus stop I realised that the 'Pay as you enter' door and steps were going to present problems.

I've no English coins, Jesus. What'll I do? I

know, this is where my veil would have come in useful!

So as the bus came I turned to an African-looking man, screwed up my face and in an imploring tone begged, 'I've just travelled back from Ireland and don't have English money, so please would you have enough to pay my fare to Streatham?'

Smiling as though the pleasure was all his, this business-suited, strong man paid my fare and put two fingers through the handle of my case and swung it safely behind the luggage rails inside the doors, almost singing in base tones, 'Anything to help a lady with a mission.'

Luckily, at the bus garage in Streatham, the driver, seeing me struggling, yanked the case out onto the oily concrete. By changing hands and stopping for breathers lots of times I eventually arrived whacked and weak at the convent gate. I looked up the path and envied the beggar. There he was seated on a stool with a tray on a folding table with a teapot on it, and he was helping himself to a long French roll, licking and turning it round his mouth to catch the ham and salad spilling over the edges. He stayed where he was and smiled at me as I struggled to open the gate and drag my case up the drive and reach over him to press the doorbell.

Dear God our Father, why am I shaking? I nearly ran this place!

'They're not likely to answer that now they're in chapel,' he chuckled, as he tore his brownish molars into his food and brushed the crumbs from what looked like a newly acquired tweed jacket.

Now, Lord, now's my chance to use my inside knowledge and give the three sharp rings signal that we Sisters used to give to signal that it was one of us.

The young woman in the new grey habit who opened the door first blinked, then stared and enquired, 'May I ask your name?'

Jesus, I want to scream, 'It is I who should be asking you for your identity! I was one of the first Sisters to clean this house years ago when we changed it from a hostel to a convent! Where were you when we fumigated and scrubbed the place from top to bottom?'

The prayers must have been over and one from the line of those leaving chapel came out to see why this aspirant was taking so long on the doorstep.

It was the Sister Superior, Sister Eileen, one of those who had pronounced her vows with me.

'Oh, so you've arrived,' she clipped through tight lips. 'Your room is above this door.' As I stepped past her she added, 'No doubt you'll want tea.' Then turning round to the girl she said, 'Put a tray in the visitors' parlour for Sister Marion Dante, will you?'

The girl gasped and putting her hand over her mouth exclaimed, 'I'm really sorry! I heard the Sisters saying your name but I didn't recognise you . . . er . . . without your veil.'

'Not your fault. How were you to know she was a Sister when she chose to hide her identity?'

I was left to lever my baggage up the two flights of stairs into a room that had been a storage space. The blind was pulled and the smell of the rubber underlay of the worn carpet took my breath away as I pushed the door open. I tugged at the blind, pulled the window up, flung myself face down on the cheap and dust-ridden candlewick cover and sobbed into its ridged, raised pattern.

Dear Jesus, this is awful. Why should I be treated like an outsider? I will not go down for the tea and biscuits to be eaten alone in the parlour!

No one came near me that awful night. Eventually I nibbled at the remainder of the ham sandwiches Sister Agnes in Maynooth had insisted on packing for me and drank water from the tap in the bathroom next door before getting into bed. I must have slept because it was dark when I opened my sore eyes and after straining my ears into the night surmised that the community had gone to bed. Afraid of suffocating, I tried to create a draught by wedging my cardigan sleeves under the door to keep it ajar and pulling the window down so that the top and bottom panes were together, letting as much air in as possible. But it was mid-August in the middle of stifling, sticky London and the room overlooked the busy road where, even as late as one in the morning, car fumes hung on the air. Decency demanded that I keep a sheet over the threadbare nightie that I had eased from the top of my case. Tossing and turning and finding that if I positioned myself on my left side my elbow would stab into me and when I lay on my back the bones in my toes knotted and intertwined. My groans woke me and I cried out. 'Oh come on! I'm tired! Please let me sleep!' It must have been tears of sheer self-pity that knocked me out long enough to snooze again.

I woke and remembered that I had no veil. I couldn't face the community without one. I wrote a note and pushed it under Sister Superior's door when the banging and the revving up of the community car assured me that they had all gone up to the Parish for Mass.

It read something like:

Dear Rev. Sister Superior,
I am sorry but I am too embarrassed to face the community because, when you met me yesterday, I realised that the Sisters in England are still wearing the full habit and I have no longer got my veil.
Please would you be able to give me a few minutes of your time this morning? I really need to be helped. I am in room 5.

Yours respectfully,
Sister Marion (Dante)

Over an hour later, after I had heard the noise of the Sisters returning from church, chatting over breakfast and then the calling out as teachers left for school, there was a knock on my door. Frightened, but delighted to receive attention, I sprang up and pulled the door open to Sister Superior.

Without looking at me she was already saying, 'I'm leaving for Liverpool in a minute but — ' Then seeing my tears she changed to, 'Come, come, pull yourself together! Nothing can be that bad, can it? One of the Sisters will loan you a veil.'

Barely able to stand, with my tissue swabbing the tears from my eyes, I cried,

207

'Please, Sister Superior, will you let me move into the flat next door? You did say this might be possible. I can't stay here any longer!'

Through the window I could see the red-bricked extension attached to the convent building that was reserved for laity, such as parents of the Sisters who might have to stay overnight. Her eyes moved from me to my unpacked case and back again.

I must have sounded pathetic as I pleaded: 'Sister Superior, I really can't take much more. Yesterday when I arrived, having somehow managed to haul my baggage from Dublin to Gatwick and then across London to here, you barely let me in. The beggar man on the doorstep was treated better.'

'I suppose it has slipped your mind that you have enjoyed two years of absence, home in your own country, and returned back here wearing only a semblance of a habit. You can hardly expect the Sisters to welcome you back with open arms!'

'In Ireland all the Sisters are much more liberated. Very few still wear the full habit. Besides you and I took our vows together. We go way back together!'

Then, softening her voice and features, Sister Superior said, 'Because you are so unsettled and unsure about your religious vocation, maybe it is better all round if you stay in the flat.' She rubbed her furrowed forehead, then quietly said, 'No doubt, if I don't concede, you'll be an even more disruptive influence on the others!' Then she added, 'This is to be a temporary arrangement, so do not envisage it lasting more than a month at the outside and should at any time the community need the rooms you are immediately to vacate them. Do I make myself clear?'

An hour later I followed the Sister in charge up the garden path. She forced opened the door of the flat and pointed to a separate lot of keys hanging on a hook inside the door saying, 'I'll come over from time to time to check that everything is kept in good order.'

She, who hailed from Galway, turned to me with smart lips and steady-set eyes from which she looked me up and down as though she thought I resembled a plucked crow. Then she said, 'I hope people seeing you coming out of here half-covered in that skimpy outfit will not think you have anything to do with us!'

After I had unpacked my bits, I went back over to the convent to find that nuns I knew, and had worked side by side with, now ignored me. From then on a weird atmosphere descended whenever I asked for food, toilet rolls, towels, to use the washing machine or for any other needs. While I had been assured that it was in order for me to eat and stay on my own, I was given no money and I was forced to ask for everything from Sisters who were preoccupied with living the style of religious life outlined in the Holy Rule of the Order.

In one instance I appeared in the dining room and tapped the shoulder of the Sister Economer (i.e. the nun who had responsibility for money matters, stationery stores etc) to ask, 'Please, Sister, could you let me have some writing paper please?'

I remember her shrugging her shoulder as if swiping a wasp and keeping her head facing out of the window she happened to be cleaning, she snapped, 'Not now! I'll leave something outside your door when I find time.'

I imagined that under the veils of all the other lowered heads in the room there was sniggering and sneering, and I backed out trying to steady my shaking hand from rattling the door handle, sniffling all the way back into my secluded flat.

I must have sat for ages just staring into space and wondering what I could do to make things better, trying to put myself in their shoes. I knew that Sister Rita still begged for almost all the food that was eaten by the community. This had become even more necessary now that very few of the Sisters were earning money, many were not trained or qualified and could not work, some were foreigners who had come to England years ago and the young people who had decided to join the congregation had to be trained. I was one of the Sisters who had been trained as a teacher and been allowed to return and gain a degree. Now I was not working and opting out of community life. Yet I knew I could not give in and go back to living a life I no longer believed in. I would have to devise a method that would not antagonise the community.

I remembered that when Sister Rita came back from the market some other Sisters would help her unload, clean and store the food down in the cellar. Those would be the best times to ask for some food but, on the other hand, she would be very busy then. It would also be embarrassing both for me and for her if I came begging in front of the other Sisters.

Write a note! That's what I'll do. I could slip it to Sister Rita without having to hang around and find an appropriate time and the right tone of voice and making sure no one was around to offend. *Why haven't I thought of this before?*

So I wrote:

Dear Sister Rita,

When it is convenient for you, please may I have the following?

Fruit and vegetables: whatever you have got.

Bread or rolls

Toilet roll

Writing paper or notelets

I know you are very busy so would it help if you put these in a box with my name on it and left it under the table at the top of the stairs coming up from the cellar?

I hope your leg is not too painful. I noticed that you are limping again.

Yours gratefully,
Sister Marion

Sister Rita had been around long enough to see many a Sister preparing to leave the Order. She exercised the art of appearing to converse when all the time she was goading you on to declare your opinions and emotions.

She would begin a conversation with something like: 'How's your brother Tim? You

212

prayed for him again last night.'

'He's back drinking again.'

'Drink's an awful thing when it gets hold of you.'

'Yes. Did you see Sister Joan emptying the bottle last night?'

'Is that right?'

'You must have noticed, Sister Rita!'

'Did someone ask her to finish it off?'

'Rita, surely you know she helps herself to the cooking wine?'

Sister Rita would put her hand over her mouth, raise her eyebrows and look surprised. We'd both giggle and she'd say nothing but I'd go on, 'I used to be shocked until that day when one of the Sisters from our headquarters in Rome came over and she was fed up with all the extra cooking and fussing about and she must have drunk a fair amount of wine before supper and she started singing a mixture of rebel songs and hymns. D'you remember the Sisters trying to get her out of the refectory and quieten her down?'

Sister Rita would go on sorting the apples, looking up from time to time to smile and nod.

'Looking back now it's funny but, at the time, when she came up the corridor later that night singing so loudly and falling about — it was so out of character. Something should have been done for her then. Sure, she was calling out for help, the poor thing!'

Both of us would pause and look, eyes wide open, at each other.

I'd continue: 'What's the use of praying for people with drink problems? Something should be done to help them. I mean we should be up front, acknowledge the problem and get them involved with AA.'

All Sister Rita would respond with was, 'D'you think so?'

I never knew where I stood with her, she was so changeable and unpredictable.

Sister Rita kept her own timetable. She got up at around five o'clock on market days, came home at about two o'clock in the afternoon to clean and store the food, then eat something, go to chapel to pray but fall asleep and retire to bed early. Because we relied on her for all our food and supplies, she was a very powerful woman.

I'd feel very guilty after being in Sister Rita's presence because I felt she was doing so much for the community and all that I had been given had been made possible by the fact that she went on working and begging day in, day out for most of her life. What motivated her? Did she still want to save souls? Did she believe she could save me?

Sister Rita's behaviour towards me also puzzled me because when she was alone with me she'd say, 'Marion, I'll be putting a wash on later on why don't you bring your smalls over and leave them by the machine?' Then she'd wink and cut up a piece of apple tart or cake and plate it for me and shove it in my hand to take back to my place. But, when Sister Superior was around me, she would bury her head down over the washing-up or look stern and serious while rubbing imaginary stains off the kitchen floor, or concentrating hard on sorting out cutlery or the like. So often I used to blame myself for setting up this strange atmosphere and question my sanity. Was I imagining that the Sisters were ignoring me or was it I who was alienating myself from them? After all, if I examined the actual words anybody used to me they would not constitute enough to convict them of unkindness.

I hated being alone and I hated being with the Sisters. My skin felt like the holes of a spider's web leaving all my nerve-ends exposed. Every time I was rebuffed it felt as though the Sisters were poking and scratching around in these holes, piercing into my being. I was constantly in spasm — suffering from shooting pains and nervous twitches from stress — and my eyes and cheeks were red raw from the continuous flowing of briny tears. Whenever I caught sight of myself in a mirror, I saw my lips resembled riverbeds eroded by a deluge. I longed to be understood and loved and yet I felt I was despised and outlawed by people I had worked alongside, dedicated to the same cause, for so many years.

It was confusing too because one day, just when I had decided that they all loathed me, a Sister knocked at my door and with a smirky smile handed me a small box of the things I had requested as she laughingly said, 'Sister Superior insisted I deliver this to you personally and inform you that she's off on her visits round our convents.' So Sister Superior had at least remembered me and was letting me know that she would not be as easily accessible should I need her.

I had tried contacting Maeve in the Battersea Community. I knew there would be too many questions if I asked permission to use the phone so I wrote her a note, managed to procure a stamp and slipped out to post it. Maeve came over to collect vegetables from Sister Rita that week and pushed a holy picture under my door while I was out with the following on it:

A Prayer of Courage
God make me brave
Help me keep Thee
In sight,
Knowing all thro' the night
That out of dark
Comes
Light.

On the back of which she scribbled: *Sometimes it is not easy to know what to do for the best. Maeve.*

★ ★ ★

The night of 18th August 1988 Sister Superior hammered at my door and I sprang from my seat to face her remarkably softened but serious expression.

Like her former self, she gently gestured to my armchair and, waiting till I was seated, said: 'Marion, it's your dad. Your mother said he has had a stroke and he's in hospital. I think you'd better go up straight away. I'll get someone to drive you to the station.'

My parents had moved back and forth to Ireland several times. They always seemed to need help and I must admit the Order had been very good to them. Through the Order they had found employment caretaking in a posh house belonging to a person who worked for the BBC and they had eventually settled in Derby.

My throat felt lumpy and tears flowed freely. I could see my father, the man who was loved by everyone who met him, and by no one more than me. The journey to Derby is a blank. Meeting my mother and sister at the hospital is blocked out. Hearing my dad's loud groans in a crowded ward is indelibly seared into my memory. A quietly confident, peace-loving man making such a din meant he was not in control. Had he gone already? Was he calling for his eldest daughter? How could a strong hearty Munsterman die?

For the following month I barely left his bedside. I talked to him, sang his song, 'The Old Bog Road', and got the nurses to sing 'When Irish Eyes Are Smiling'. I mopped his brow. I prayed and got the Parish Priest to bless and pray over him. I blame heightened emotions and tension for leading me to fight in turn with my brothers and sisters, even my mother. My hero was dying and I was convinced that I was special to him. It was not until his funeral though that I discovered that each of us felt he had a unique place for each one in his heart. Had that been his secret touch? Making each of us feel that we were his favourite?

I wished once more that we were better off and had enough money. Dad should have been buried in St Joseph's Church back in Limerick. His forebears had built that church and the family lived off O'Connell Street, round the corner from it. The middle child in a family of seven, he was much loved. Because he did not appear to be restricted by convention or social class, he acted with great freedom. For instance, as a young girl I remember him taking me by the hand up the middle aisle to the front bench of the big Jesuit church one Sunday. To do this he had to walk past the men at the door holding out plates to collect silver coins from the well-off and to ignore the reserved signs on the kneelers for wealthy benefactors. He said nothing to anybody and nobody questioned him. Thus he put aside the custom of worshippers entering through separate church doors according to whether they gave copper or silver contributions.

I thought I would never stop crying when my father died and I was so weak that I could barely walk or keep any food down. Many days I wanted to stay in bed forever. But sometimes I sensed Dad's freedom and longed to begin again. I had always felt that he had not really wanted me to become a nun.

* ★ ★

In October 1988, a month after we had buried him, I was offered an opportunity to sort my life out in Kingfisher Therapeutic Centre for the Religious.

Having made an appointment to see Mother Provincial, I was now seated in her office in Chertsey. Gone was the polished table that in the past would have separated us. Instead now we both sat in armchairs and I was invited to pull mine nearer.

'Now, Marion, having discussed your state of health and the uncertainty that you still seem to experience after two years in Ireland, the Superiors have concluded that I should offer further help.'

Great! My innards have been taken out for dissection! What about confidentiality and privacy?

She must have sensed my feelings so she explained. 'You understand that I have to justify the amount of money that needs to be spent on any Sister, but that does not necessitate my disclosing private confidences discussed between us.'

My breathing slowed down at the same time as my shoulders fell back into place and I confessed, 'I was worried.'

'Now, Sister Marion, I am going to entrust

220

you with information I will ask you to keep to yourself because it concerns the privacy of other Sisters. Will you promise to keep what I say to you within these walls?'

Relieved and curious, I bent forward assuring her, 'Of course!'

She then told me that there were other Sisters who were in a similar position to me and fortunately the Council of Major Superiors in recognition of this type of need had succeeded in setting up two centres in this country where Religious could go for help.

'Do you think you would benefit from this kind of help?'

I felt surprised yet I put my head down and a tissue under my glasses to catch my seeping tears, and in a shaky voice I managed, 'Yes.'

'Marion, I want to help you.' She leaned forward towards me and then, opening up the folder on her lap, continued in softer tones. 'Look, I have the two brochures here and having read through them I actually think the one that is more expensive would suit you better. That's because this one is more community-based and, in the other one, in Southampton, you would be treated on a one-to-one basis. But the decision is yours. Take the brochures away with you and think it over.'

Snuggling my elbows into my sides and resting my head on my hands, I blinked my tears away enough to notice her eyes glisten before she uttered words I have ever since treasured.

'Marion, I want you to be as happy as you can ever be in this world. After all you have been through lately you may not be able to believe that this is possible, but it is. I wish I could give you some of the contentment I really feel inside me but you know I can't so I am determined to get you the help I think will do you good. Even if you could be happy for one day I would be at peace. Whether you decide to leave us or to stay doesn't really matter.'

On every occasion since that I recalled those words I have been moved.

Then torrents of tears gushed down my face as I grabbed the tissues she was holding out to me. Once more I marvelled at her kindness and wondered why more money was being promised to help me.

Mother Provincial had explained to me that these two centres, one outside Birmingham and the other in Southampton, were kept as secret destinations mainly because many of the priests and nuns going there felt that there was a stigma attached to needing this kind of help. Would mental illness be equated with madness? I also had a vested interest in maintaining secrecy about the year in Kingfisher House because my mother had suffered from a mental breakdown after the birth of my brother and, although this may well have been diagnosed as postnatal depression nowadays, back then it discredited her.

21

Kingfisher House

In autumn 1988, just after my father had died, I pulled my case off the Euston to Birmingham train at Birmingham International. I had met Sister Julian a week before when I had gone for my interview, so we reached out to each other immediately. She pressed her warm cheek against mine and once in her clutches I felt safe. She said very little as she drove out into the country and up a long avenue through crunching rich autumn leaves till we parked at the entrance to the red-bricked mansion that is Kingfisher House, the therapeutic centre for priests and nuns. A tall smiling man with long sturdy arms grasped my case. Sister Julian led the way up the wide, red-patterned, carpeted stairs into a fairly big room that seemed to have everything. The curtains, bed covers and armchair upholstery were a wine colour. There was a built-in wardrobe, a sink, a desk and an armchair too.

As I moved further into the room, I looked through the half-open window, and noticed copper-brown leaves clinging to the beeches and I longed to snuggle into bed and sleep my pain away.

Dear Jesus, maybe I'll find peace here? Dad, are you too taking care of me?

As it was then half past six and dinner was at seven. I barely had time to splash water on my face before Sister Julian returned to take me down to a spacious dining room with what seemed like thirty men and women seated round an oval-shaped table.

'I'm sure you'd like to welcome Sister Marion.' Then bending down and catching hold of her elbow, in a quieter voice she addressed a grey-haired woman in a blue brushed-wool cardigan with, 'Maybe you could show her the ropes tonight. Would you mind?'

With that, the skinny woman uncoiled from her seat to pull out the chair next to hers and squash me in between her and an older man who seemed to be so fragile that a teaspoon might knock him over.

I was asked how my journey was and which room I was in, but I was aware from the start that no personal details were being exchanged. Then I remembered I had been told that *'while any client can elect to tell as little or as much about themselves as they choose, it is not to be taken for granted that* other persons might want to divulge their identities. These safeguards are assured in order that people availing themselves of this type of therapy should feel secure in a protected environment.'

As we waited for dinner to be served there was no mistaking that roast chicken was on the menu. Sure enough, after our melon and blackcurrant starter, the tasty bird was served with both boiled and roast potatoes together with broccoli and carrots. For dessert we had caramel pudding and then there was coffee or tea. Bowls of seasonal fruit were within reach and baskets of brown and white rolls, together with jugs of iced water and real orange juice. I had not eaten so much food for ages.

I was not sure whether the man with what I thought of as a television face sitting opposite me was a priest or a Brother. He seemed to front one direction at a time, screen what was happening and then swivel round to gather data from another angle. When I became aware that he had fixed on me I wondered what I looked like now.

Dear Lord, I suspect that all my worrying has wrinkled my skin so much that nobody will want to be near me, let alone be attracted to me.

★　★　★

I went to the toilet three times before the nine a.m. community meeting. From the bathroom window I could see the men and women whom I knew to be nuns, priests or Brothers walking up and down pathways bordered with manicured beds of bright flowers underneath bronzed autumn foliage. So many splashes of colour in nature and in the clothes worn in this new community made me blink. I flushed the loo again and clung to the banister as I made my way down to say hello to the woman I had been introduced to the night before.

On the dot of nine everyone made their way through two open doors to sit on armchairs arranged in a circle round a big room. The talking quieted down and Father Jerry, the psychotherapist, who had interviewed me a few days before, looked across and said,

'Sister Marion, as I explained to you previously, it is the custom here for new arrivals to introduce themselves to this community informing us why it is you feel that you could benefit by being here in Kingfisher House. You have already agreed that confidentiality and due respect for the identity of individuals attending this type of therapeutic centre is essential to the proper functioning of all concerned. So welcome,

Sister Marion . . . I understand you prefer to be known as 'Marion', is that so?'

All the faces were blurred into upturned shades of pink. My cheeks burnt and the tissues in my hands dampened as I stammered, 'Yes, I usually get called Marion. I'm Irish. I'm a teacher and my dad has just died . . . ' Then my throat dried up so that when I tried to swallow it seemed to lever a pump in my eyes, releasing rivulets of tears. My trembling fingers fumbled at my sleeve and an unknown woman beside me thrust tissues on my lap. Sniffling and sobs from almost everybody started at once and continued for a few minutes before Father Jerry's deep sonorous tones anchored us as he invited, 'Would it help if you told us who you are crying for, Tessa?'

A squashed cranberry face next to Father Jerry tilted itself back and a howling cry spluttered out, followed by yet more sobbing.

'Take your time. Let it come. Don't hold back now, Tessa!' Father Jerry put his hand on her shoulder and turned his face in nearer to her.

Then there was a little whimper from someone too near for me to see, while many others with heads down reached to pull tissues from the box that was being passed around the circle.

Dear God, why are they using my father's death as an excuse to indulge in their private grief?

I straightened my legs and banged my heels into the cherry carpet, wiped my glasses and pouched my lips.

Then Father Jerry's eyes caught mine and he shouted across, 'Tessa's dad was a great man!'

I screamed aloud, 'My father was the greatest man that ever walked this earth!' I glared round the circle then splattered massive tears, heaved loud sobs into soggy tissues and dropped my head onto my chest.

My heart thumped into the silence as I longed for them all to get on with the meeting and let me be with my dad — my big strong Munster dad, slowly and painfully being eased into death with morphine in his hospital bed.

'You love your dad,' said Father Jerry.

I swallowed hard and closed my eyes but the salty tears streamed down to my lips, chin and neck as I rocked myself.

There was a very long pause and gradually I opened my eyes to see the shoes of those near me and feel as though I had been cradled after my outcry.

Then a gentle woman's voice whispered across the circle, 'What was your dad like?'

I rested my head back into my neck socket and still catching tears on my quivering lips, I tried to explain. 'Everybody loved my dad. He was kind and loved by everyone and was a gentle giant with smiling eyes . . . ' By opening and closing my eyes I began to flick the torrents of tears trickling down and catch them on my tongue. 'He loved each one of his five children. We each know we are special to him for different reasons. Oh, if he walked in here now you would all just love him!'

After this first community meeting on the day I began my stay in Kingfisher House, Sister Breda called me into her office. She was in charge and worked alongside five psychotherapists and other members of staff. I was told that I would go to Father Jerry twice a week for a one-to-one psychotherapy session.

When I was given the timetable I discovered that each day was structured around the Divine Office or Liturgy of the Hours, adhered to by most Religious Orders: Lauds (or Morning Prayer), None, Vespers, Compline (or Night Prayer).

The big difference in Kingfisher House, though, was that all manner of therapies were available to enable each one of us to try to come to grips with whatever would help us as we struggled to ponder on what had hitherto prevented us from living a fulfilled life. This constant analysing, examining and evaluating, however, can be very demanding on those who are already suffering psychological pain.

Each day we walked up and down the well-kept paths and through beautifully manicured gardens before the community meetings that began promptly at nine a.m. Then we followed each other into the big room where a selection of upright and more comfortable quasi-armchairs were arranged in a circle.

Most days I felt exhilarated and convinced that the various psychotherapists, psychiatrists, art therapists who sat and worked among us to guide and support us were an excellent team of experts and that we were privileged to be given this professional help.

No two community meetings were the same. They revealed so much but they could be gruelling and exacting.

Here's what happened at one:

'Marion, why are you acting like a three-year-old wheeling yourself in on a tricycle between the adults?' enquired Breda after I had selfishly interrupted two other residents struggling to come to grips with their loss of siblings at a very early age.

Some of the residents turned bulldog faces towards me. Others raised upturned hands as

231

if exasperated. Did I detect devilment in one pair of laughing eyes? And one person glared a daring look. I lowered my head while I questioned my motives.

Why had I regressed? Was I trying to block their discussion? What relevance did this topic have in my life? Was I looking for attention or was there something subconsciously going on for me? As a result of this probing and examining I was quick to extract that part of the remark that was relevant for me.

'I want to be three or better two. I was never really a child. I had to grow up and help too quickly and now I want to regress and have fun and play. What's wrong with that?'

I heard Breda say, 'OK. Go back. Where are you? What can you see?'

I started to feel the tears trickling down my cheeks. 'I'm under the table. It's cold concrete and Mammy's crying and talking to herself in between the sobs.'

'How do you feel? Are you frightened?'

'Why is she crying again?' I wailed.

The therapy continued and moved to others in the group.

Then when an hour had elapsed the therapists went in the middle to review what happened while we the residents listened and tried to glean what would help us in our self-assessment.

'Marion seems to like pulling things asunder and examining them,' observed a psychotherapist.

Later in a one-to-one psychotherapy session with Father Jerry I came to realise that if I was not careful I could develop an obsession with analysing everything. Eventually as the fifty minutes allocated to this session progressed I told Father Jerry that what I felt was like an urge to pull up a beautiful flower by its roots just to see how it grew, resulting in the stunting of its growth and being deprived of its beauty.

In spite of being aware of my compulsion to probe and dig deep, I became a catalyst at the community meetings. Having learnt to fathom my mother's ravings at such a young age, I discovered that being privy to what made the other thirty clients tick was wonderful material to work with. Of course I made many mistakes at guessing and prejudging other clients' motives. I antagonised many but this was grist to the mill in Kingfisher House where every statement and action could be used in evidence against you. However, as the people who had elected to reside in this therapeutic centre chose to use this type of process to sort and mend their broken lives, they learnt to use the situations for their own healing progress.

When Susie took us for psychodrama we were given the opportunity of plumbing the depths of our subconscious motivation.

'What's that book you are ripping to pieces with such vigour, Marion?'

It was a copy of the Yellow Pages phone book yet I answered without hesitation: 'The Rule Book.'

'Why are you tearing it apart?'

'I'm fed up of rules. There's any amount of them and I hate them! I want to be free of them. Why can't I do what I like when I feel like doing it?'

At the same time as I became more determined to make myself a better person, I hungered for the constant support of my psychotherapist Father Jerry. I wanted to collapse into total dependency on him. However, as this was a common tendency with clients he was forearmed and forewarned, prepared and thoroughly professional. He knew all about transference so when I declared my undying love for him he recognised my tremendous and unquestioning love for my father. In this total proclamation of love I continually placed my father on a pedestal. So too Father Jerry could do no wrong, whereas I tended to be much more critical of Breda, the mother figure at the centre of the life I had now substituted for my own natural family.

I realised early on that I was very fortunate and grateful that the Salesian Congregation did not count the cost when Mother Provincial encouraged me to go to Kingfisher House. Hopefully, in spite of my many limitations, having been privy to what makes a small cross-section of the population tick has broadened my understanding and helped me to be a little more tolerant.

The only shortcoming many of us felt about Kingfisher House was in its aftercare or lack thereof. The constant analysing, examining and evaluating proved to be very demanding on those of us who were still suffering psychological pain when they were released back into everyday society.

Later I was further disillusioned to find that it was also in the religious superiors' interest to keep people from realising the therapeutic centres existed because they were so costly, and if every member of their Order who questioned their vocation requested to go there the coffers would soon be heavily depleted. The fact, too, that a large proportion of those who went there soon left their religious way of life put them on their guard. Eventually, I heard that both Kingfisher House and the other centre near Southampton were closed down.

22

Released Back into the Community

I asked to go to our community house in Battersea because my friend Maeve was there.

During the fifteen months I spent in Kingfisher House I often tried to imagine what it would be like being back in the community.

But that first Monday morning in May I prayed:

Dear Jesus, if only I could sit in the circle meetings and let my feeling 'hang out'. I need Father Jerry's care and understanding. In spite of the fact that he tried to prepare me for separation, I still feel so lost without him. Here I've got to be so controlled.

The Battersea creamy brown armchair had a hard frame but sagging bottom.

Mary my Mother, help me to sit up straight, keep my feet on the ground and look like a nun. How can I hide my scary feelings though? I'm like an egg without its shell.

There was only Sister Maureen and myself in this comparatively new convent that from the outside looked like two ordinary semi-detached houses. No one, except perhaps the postman, would know that number six and eight, near the one-way system on this very busy road, were owned by nuns. The blinds on the front window prevented outsiders from seeing that the elongated light-blue-carpeted front room was set aside as a chapel. They could not admire the intricate silver workmanship of the tabernacle attached to the wall at eye level. The golden flicker from the lamp burning perpetually to remind all of the real presence of Jesus was usually hidden behind a beautiful arrangement of lilies and shades of yellow and orange freesia and such like.

'*Viva Gesu* (Long live Jesus), Sister Marion,' greeted seventy-year-old Sister Maureen.

'*Viva Maria* (Long live Mary)!' I responded as we brushed past each other in the doorway.

All the others were at work while I was seated in the community room surrounded by a mini-library of spiritual reading and biographies of saints. On an MFI self-assembly coffee table I had spread out the local newspaper so as to cover over the letter that Mother Provincial had handed me the night before.

After Kingfisher House everything seemed cheap, trying to be cheerful and too clean.

Where there might have been frivolous ornaments there were plastic images of the Pope, Saint John Bosco and Saint Mary Mazzarello. There were no smells, just polluted Battersea air allowed in through a ventilator in the wall.

At six o'clock that morning I had turned over when the bell to waken the other five sisters in this house had rung. I heard them moving about in silence, taking turns in the bathroom and going downstairs to begin prayers at seven o'clock. At 7:45 a.m. a priest must have come to say Mass because I heard singing. Luckily, since I had been given the spare room at the back of the house I was oblivious to any other noise until they chatted at breakfast. I turned over in my single, iron-framed bed and pulled the skimpy duvet and faded nylon green sheets up carefully so as not to bump myself or the bed against three of the walls. I gauged the time by the increasing light coming through the skylight window. I reluctantly opened my eyes to my pasty cream surroundings. From floor to ceiling had been painted or covered in an anaemic shade and, although there was carpet, the pile was so brittle that it might as well have been bare boards.

I avoided going down until they had all gone out to school. The night before, Maeve did not seem to be as friendly as I had known her to be. However, she told me that she and another Sister were teaching in a school near enough to walk to and that Sister Alice was in charge of this community as well as being the headmistress of the state aided Catholic primary school.

Dear God, I want to tear up this letter! Why is Mother Provincial telling me that I have to make up my mind by April? One year to decide the rest of my life! It's true these nuns have been good to me. I can't deny that, but why do I feel that they expect me to go the way of all those who have been through this process and leave? I hurt and maybe they feel betrayed. What was it Sister Kathie told me privately? 'Fair enough, you are considering whether you can live with us any more, but think — how does that make us feel?'

To satisfy this agreement I had to find suitable accommodation and try out what it would be like to live outside the community. The arrangement was that I would be given one hundred pounds a month and my flat or bed-sit would be paid. According to church rule, detailed in Canon Law, I would still be bound by my three vows of poverty, chastity and obedience until such time as I asked and it be agreed that I was officially dispensed from these promises. This meant that my teaching salary continued to be paid into the Order, I was not supposed to be looking for a relationship and I still took instructions from the Superiors of the Order.

How am I going to cope, Jesus? Everything here is so different to Kingfisher House. I'm sneaking about. I don't feel at home.

The kitchen was clinically clean. There was not even a trace of a crumb anywhere. The tinny sink was stainless and everything in the fridge was orderly. To one side of the cupboard there were little packets of cereal in a plastic labelled container and six matching bowls, plates, saucers etc neatly stacked. Perfection!

I carefully poured semi-skimmed milk from the opened carton on to my cornflakes and was frightened to sit down in case I didn't put the chair back into the position it had been in and I held my bowl over the sink so that any splash would run away. Then, having washed my bowl and replaced it, I opened the folding doors into the community room.

I was supposed to be scanning the local newspaper for accommodation. I had been instructed to get something for around £50 a week. I hadn't a clue what to do and I felt that if anyone should prod my flimsy skin, it would burst and I would spill all over the place.

The double-glazing kept out most of the traffic noise from the road via Battersea to Clapham Junction, but I could hear Sister Maureen pottering around next door, picking up the post from the cheap black rubber-backed mat and watering the flowers in chapel. Even though she was retired, she had her jobs:

to manage the community finances;
translate from Italian to English short biographies of Sisters who had died;
prepare the meals;
do various other chores like shopping and answering the phone and collecting pre-scriptions from the surgery.

Sister Maureen came in to replace a book on the shelf behind me. She didn't even make eye contact so I went on pretending that I was circling bed-sits and flats in the local paper.

Dear Jesus, why is Sister Maureen not talking to me? Is she keeping a check on me? She's so like those bishops and priests in the photographs and paintings in the corridor in Maynooth Rogues' Gallery! All still, stately and dead! Those distinguished folk who didn't want people to enjoy themselves.

The trickling of the running water in the kitchen brought me back from my wanderings. I rubbed my eyes and tried to focus on the industrial brownish, mottled carpet.

The bell rang at exactly the same time that the hall clock chimed twelve. That was the signal for prayers and even though there were only two of us in the house, Sister Maureen expected me to join her for the examination of conscience.

She shuffled into chapel and start reciting, '*In the name of the Father and of the Son and of the Holy Spirit.*'

Following behind her, I wondered what she could possibly have done to offend the Almighty during the course of that morning. But then, if she felt as guilty about wasting time daydreaming and was as burdened as I was with seeking perfection, maybe she was also suffering from guilt and so needed to confess to Jesus Christ, Our Divine Redeemer.

We prayed as though there was an entire community present and then we sat at either end of the Formica-covered round table and ate the tomato soup and cheese on toast prepared by this seventy-year-old Sister. The seersucker serviettes in rings with our names punched onto a plastic base were stored in the table drawer together with blue raffia place mats. Our tinny cutlery was in place. She had a hearing loss and so she did not say much, but she blew her nose very loudly into her big discoloured handkerchief. We used to say she 'flew the flag' because she still wore the full-length black habit and the bonnet and long veil. She had refused to get new specs and so probably was not aware that the front of her cape and her long sleeves had a few greasy spots and the rubber heels of her grey-striped slippers were worn down. Because she had once been Sister Superior I did not feel at ease in her company and, as it was known that I was about to leave religious life, I wondered if she who had adhered to the strict living of the Rule would be able to sympathise with me in my present plight. But the more I reflected on the kind of life this institutionalised old woman had lived the more I wanted to get away and live the life I still valued.

We went through the routine of eating, washing, drying and putting the crockery away in silence. We omitted having the half an hour recreation period together but we went into chapel again to make our visit to the Blessed Sacrament. She read all the prayers, probably believing that I was praying beside her.

Back in the community room I struggled with sleep that afternoon.

Then I heard the slamming of car doors.

Dear Lord, it can't be that late! Another day and what have I done?

I dreaded the, 'How did you get on today?' when Maeve came in from school. Did she mean, 'How long more are you going to be without a job?' or 'Have you come to your senses and realised by now that you are incapable of looking after yourself?'

What was I to do? They knew I had not responded to the rising bell and probably guessed that I had no longer any inclination to pray. Fortunately, I had not told anyone that I hated having breakfast with them before they rushed off to teach because I wondered if they resented me eating food I had not earned. I asked myself, did they expect me to go to prayers and wear the habit? Why couldn't they see things the way I saw them now? I ached from head to toe and longed to be understood.

It must be four o'clock, I realised, because that was when the Sisters arrived home from teaching. No matter how tired they were they would keep to the routine of having tea, reciting the Rosary, reading from their spiritual reading books and retiring to their rooms to prepare next day's lessons until a bell rang at five to six. I remember one afternoon when it was 'that time of the month' I just fell asleep in chapel and snored so loudly that I had to be woken up and told to go to bed.

Usually though, discipline was recommended and, as the Rule book stated, *'the silence which is the fruit of interior and exterior self-control and productive of personal union with God and growth in the virtues necessary in community life . . . is encouraged.'*

So there was to be no raucous laughing or hilarity!

Sister Maeve looked over my shoulder at the local paper. 'Any luck?' she asked, pointing to the 'To Let' column and the three addresses I'd circled in red.

'No.'

'What did they say?'

'I didn't get round to phoning. I thought I'd wait 'til the cheaper rate kicked in, besides I wondered if they would be too far away.'

'From what?'

'Will you help me?' I asked.

Maeve nodded.

I felt so relieved that Maeve seemed to be her old self again.

Taking a chance I admitted, 'Maeve, I'm frightened.'

Pulling the door to, she smiled saying, 'I've missed you.'

'Oh Maeve!' I cried as I hugged her. 'Oh Maeve, you don't know how much I longed for us to be together again!' I hugged her again.

Eventually, freeing herself from our embrace, she said, 'Tell me what's worrying you.'

'Oooh . . . where do I begin? Well, for starters, I haven't got the teaching post I've applied for yet.'

She smiled and kept her hand on my shoulder as I beamed back. 'You will. Remember you are an excellent teacher. Think about all those happy successful children that have been through your classes. You know you can do it again. But tell me more?' She sat down, putting her legs over the side of the chair.

'It's such little things. Silly little things like having to find my way about on buses and trains again. Me,' I said, pointing a finger at myself, 'who drove Superiors and foreign students, everyone everywhere over the years. There's so much I'm beginning to realise I've haven't thought through.'

Maeve coughed and opened and closed the folding doors, checking to make sure there was no one in the chapel next door. She sat and moved her chair closer.

I trembled a little, took off my cardigan. 'Maeve, this August I should be celebrating my silver jubilee and from now on enjoying a few of the perks I have earned over the years.'

'Perks?'

246

She opened her arms wide and turned up her palms.

'You have to agree that I would be certain to be looked after in my old age over in our retirement home in Cowley?'

'You're only forty-something! A mere babe! Besides, by the time you get to that ripe old age of let's say seventy, there might not be anyone left to look after you. At the rate we're going at the moment, our numbers will be down soon enough.'

Maeve was wrinkling her eyebrows up.

'So you don't think I'm making a big mistake?'

'You and all the others,' she laughed. 'Besides, haven't you had time to think? What's this place Kingfisher House?'

'How d'you know about that? That's supposed to be hush-hush. Do all that lot know?' I opened the top button of my blouse.

'Keep your hair on. I wouldn't be sure, all I know is that Sister Amelia accidentally spilled the beans on where her sister was and many of us are curious because where you were was top secret too.'

Drawing my chair closer and placing my hands on hers, I confided, 'What goes on in Kingfisher House is confidential and I was promised that it would be kept that way. It was all very good, while painful, and some day I'll tell you more. But please keep it to yourself, will you?'

'I'm sorry. I had no intention of adding to your stress. Are you too upset to come to chapel?'

'I'd better turn up if I don't want to draw too much attention to myself.' I blew my nose and tidied myself. 'I'm off to the loo and then I'll join you.'

'When the community comes out from Vespers it will be past six and it will be cheaper to phone then,' smiled Maeve.

I turned so she did not see my eyes brimming with tears. Why was she being so kind to me?

I opened my *A to Z of London* in chapel in order to locate some of the accommodation addresses and realized that once again my eyes had begun to sting and my eyelids glue together, preventing me from seeing properly, so I just mumbled through the psalms.

★ ★ ★

The phone box was under the stairs and it was a squash to fit two of us in, so I agreed to hold the door open and hold the bit of the newspaper with the number and details close enough to Maeve while she dialled.

'Who will I say I am?' she asked.

248

'Better just use your own name and make out you're enquiring for your friend Marion.'

'No, that won't work. No, I'll pretend I'm you.'

'Right, good idea, less complications. Try this one first because it is the cheapest and my sister was born in Clapham South and it is on the Northern Line.'

'Here goes. 0703 . . . it's ringing. Hello, I'm enquiring about the flat you have advertised in the *South London News*. Oh! So it's gone. Thank you.'

We took turns and tried two more and the third was a Mrs Poliskie who answered after just two rings and sounded as Polish as her name. Maeve put her hand over the phone and whispered, 'She says she can show us round tonight at seven thirty. Is that OK?'

I nodded my assent.

'Right, the flat is actually on Balham High Street and, yes, we will meet you outside Barclays Bank at seven thirty.' She put the receiver down saying, 'That gives us time to join the others for supper and then I'll drive you there or perhaps you can drive since you know your way about that area.'

I ate hardly anything and felt so out of place as the Sisters discussed what had gone on in their various classrooms that day. Then, having asked Sister Superior for permission and explained where we wanted to go and checked that no one else needed the use of the car that evening, we were both excused from helping with the washing-up and went to get ready.

Maeve arrived down wearing 'ordinary' clothes because she said she thought that it would be easier if she accompanied me without her habit so that I needn't disclose too much about myself.

'Your hair is in good shape,' I remarked.

'Mrs O' Driscoll, the mother of one of the pupils, is a hairdresser,' Maeve said, running her fingers through her fringe. 'She offered! I couldn't resist!'

'I like your denim skirt, where did you get that?' I asked, pulling my beige jacket over a white cotton blouse and pleated skirt.

'Our Claire let me borrow it when we went on holiday and then she said I could keep it. Goes well with this jacket, do you think?'

'Looks like a complete outfit what with those matching blue shoes,' I complimented her.

Having gone to school myself years ago in Tooting Broadway, I found my way to Balham and easily located the bank. We had arrived ten minutes early and waited for Mrs Poliskie. She arrived in a BMW on the dot of seven thirty and looked very smart in an olive-green trouser suit as she came to introduce herself.

Formalities over, we followed her through a door up a flight of twenty stairs into a self-contained furnished flat which was basically one big room divided in half into a bedroom and kitchen separated by a tiny toilet and shower room. But it was well-lit, had everything and was clean and smelt of the light blue paint. The central heating was included in the £60 a week rent and the previous tenant had left the phone. Of course it would be up to me to have it reconnected.

When she had shown us round Mrs Poliskie waited and looking at me said, 'Well, are you interested? I have had a young man around and he is to let me know one way or the other by nine in the morning, but quite honestly I have had a succession of men who have moved on so quickly lately and I am tired of all this chopping and changing.'

I felt so scared. The whole idea of being unprotected on my own was beginning to dawn on me. Then I heard myself saying, 'The thing is, I am just deciding if I should leave the convent and this is the first flat I have looked at and I'm not sure what I should do.'

Maeve looked as though a bomb had exploded and Mrs Poliskie's eyes opened

251

wide before she said, 'Why didn't you explain this on the phone? I have a bedsit I let out to students in my own house in Wimbledon and if you like you're welcome to come over tomorrow and look at it. Maybe that would suit you better. I am a Catholic myself and I'm sure we could work things out.'

Thank you, Jesus! Thank you very much!

I felt so relieved and arranged to travel over to 50 Moonshine Road for midday the following day. When we got back into the car I apologised big time to Maeve for blowing her cover, but she assured me she was glad in the end that I had explained my real circumstances to Mrs Poliskie.

Mrs and Mr Poliskie and their sixteen-year-old son Mark had a beautiful detached house in a highly desirable residential area of Wimbledon. I had travelled on two buses and located the address very easily. As I approached Number 50 I was delighted to realise that this fairly modern house with the bay windows was situated in a quiet upmarket cul-de-sac. I opened the wooden gate in the fence that surrounded a well-kept garden, entered the red-tiled porch shaded by wisteria and rang the shining brass doorbell. I could see Mrs Poliskie approaching as I looked through the stained-glass panels in the dark oak door and I prayed, '*Thanks again, Lord, for looking after me!'*

There she was, dressed casual to smart in crushed off-white linen trousers and an open-necked pale pink top. Her flyaway hairstyle was attractive around a sallow complexion and her fluffy pink slippers amused me as she led the way upstairs, smiling while she welcomed me into her home.

'I'm sure you want to see your room,' she said as she opened the glowing white door of a back bedroom, which overlooked a beautiful long cultivated garden. The white paintwork glistened and wine was the colour that pervaded the matching floral curtains, upholstery and duvet covering. My feet sank into the pile of the carpet. I was very pleased that I would have a separate bathroom and toilet next door and a key to my bedroom and one to the front door.

I had no hesitation in accepting this accommodation and simply let the Sister Economer and my landlady make their own arrangements about paying my rent. Two days later I moved into my Wimbledon bed-sit. Sister Maeve easily transported my few belongings by car. I had been given two pairs of mended white sheets from the community stock, a used bath towel and two smaller towels, two face flannels and a hot-water bottle. Mrs Poliskie provided me with a kettle, pots and a pan and everything else.

On the day after I moved in I received a letter telling me that I had been successful in obtaining a teaching post in a Catholic primary school in Battersea. What more could I want?

Everything was new to me. I had never kept money before, I was still not used to wearing ordinary clothes and it was ages since I had cooked for myself. I was sent the agreed one hundred pounds which was to last me a month and be used to buy food, transport, phone calls and for the laundrette.

I got used to putting my soiled clothes into one of those £1 red-white-and-blue-checked plastic holdalls with a handle and zip on a Friday evening or early on a Saturday morning and heading for the laundrette. It was less busy then and I would be more likely to be able to get a machine. I travelled by bus to the laundrette opposite Raynes Park railway station.

I sometimes had to wait twenty minutes with my bus pass in one hand and the other at the ready to haul my washing on board. This got worse in the winter months. I sometimes had to fight back tears as I dismounted, struggling with my washing and crossing by the lights into the steamy laundrette. I learnt that I could reduce the cost by bringing my own washing powder. Armed with the exact coins needed to insert in the machine I'd put my load in, press the appropriate buttons, calculate the amount of time it would take and go out and around the corner to the two phone boxes to make essential phone calls. I could not afford the luxury of phoning friends, or often even my family, because all my ten and twenty-pence coins disappeared far too quickly.

Reluctantly I would return to the depressing steamy laundrette. I often tried to read, but I disliked the gloomy assortment of early-morning faces and the smells and noise so much that my spirit always sank and I resolved that the first thing I would buy when I had the money was a washing machine. Once, when I had returned five minutes after my machine had finished, a man had tugged all my belongings out and dumped them on a dirty table next to the driers. When I saw the scrawny old fellow who was culpable of mauling my private undies, I was so put off that I said nothing and went home without spinning them. But I soon regretted doing this when I became aware that my damp load was heavier on the bus and very hard to dry on white radiators in my bedroom. I hoped I would succeed before the steam discoloured my fine lace curtains or Mrs Poliskie noticed that I was wasting the heating by having the top of the windows opened in November.

Alone, I was very frightened. Even though I had experienced nothing but kindness from my landlady, I locked my room door and listened out for every noise especially from the landlady's son. I had never been so close to a male. I think he resented me being there because, soon after I had moved in when she had gone out, he played his music so loudly that I had to ask him to turn it down. That particular night I was amazed to sense the thumping beat coming up through the ceiling. I was already in bed by ten o'clock, because I had to be down at the corner each morning to catch the seven twenty-five bus to Wimbledon station. I tried turning over and pulling my pillow closer round by my ears, but it was the thumping of the rhythm that seemed to penetrate into my very being. Then I got out of bed and banged the heel of my shoe on the ceiling and waited. The music seemed to get louder, so I unlocked my door and banged it closed. I realised just how loud the racket was when I opened the door so I pulled on my dressing-gown and marched straight down the stairs and banged on the door that led into the Poliskie household. A dishevelled Mark opened up and stared surprised at me.

I suspected he had been drinking and said pleadingly, 'Your music is keeping me awake and I have an early start in the morning.'

'Is that so?' he said and slammed the door to. But he turned the music down.

Hours later I awoke screaming, convinced that a hand had come through the bedroom wall to strangle me.

Mrs Poliskie, the landlady, was a good cook and, when the smells wafted around the house, hunger pangs raged and I pined for care and nourishment. As I didn't have a fridge I had to buy daily and I hadn't a clue what to buy and imagined that everybody was watching me going round and round in Sainsbury's comparing prices, wondering what would last, considering how to cook the food. It took so much time and energy. A big pan loaf was cheaper but I was so embarrassed when I had to smuggle out half-mouldy slices into Mrs Poliskie's bin. The same applied to the milk except it would go off sooner. If I bought more than I could carry, I would add to the cost by having to get on the bus.

Then, belatedly, I discovered that was not the case since I possessed a zone ticket. *Whoopee!*

Church was like a comfort blanket for me in my utter loneliness. I chose to go to the Sacred Heart Church in Wimbledon which was run by Jesuits. I respected them as priests who perform their duties well and know how to organise and run a parish efficiently, but also as intellectuals who would challenge my thinking. So, with little else to distract me from teaching and having abandoned the ritual of daily Mass, I dressed up to go to church on Sundays despite the fact that I was questioning all that went on there. I suppose I had been institutionalised so long I needed to keep to some discipline and routine and, in any case, what else could I do on a Sunday that cost little and where I might meet others? So I grabbed the comfort blanket with all its familiar smells!

★ ★ ★

The first Sunday I was in my new flat I woke up early and marvelled at the silence. The sun was bright in the heavens at seven o'clock. I waited, listening to birds chirping and insects nattering for half an hour and then the bells from the Sacred Heart Church got me creeping out of bed. I only had three skirts to choose from to wear. Maeve had given me a pink blouse a few days before, so I decided on the navy skirt with the pink carnations to go with it. What clothes I possessed I had chosen to replace my habit and so they had plenty of material in the skirts and the more voluminous the top the more comfortable I felt. I would not even consider anything that was figure-hugging, still being restricted by concepts of modesty, purity, and asexual appeal. Also, living in the same house as a young man and in a conservative area of Wimbledon made me more self-conscious. My beloved olive trousers were abandoned long since, together with the wonderful freedom I had experienced back in Dublin!

I ran as little water as possible so that I would not disturb my landlady's family, dressed quietly and put on my navy-blue blazer jacket and the only pair of flat black sandals that I possessed.

The streets were empty apart from the few walking their dogs or heading in the same direction as I was. As I climbed the hill, crossed the road and walked up the leafy path to this awesome spired church, I realized that no one knew me. Whereas before my habit had distinguished me from other worshippers, now no-one opened the door for a badly dressed middle-aged woman. They certainly did not incline their heads saying 'Good morning, Sister'.

Feeling self-conscious and not adequately dressed, I blessed myself with Holy Water, elected to sit midway up the church, genuflected and knelt beside a young couple with a gorgeous blonde three-year-old girl, wearing a flimsy pale-pink dress that gave the appearance of being overlapping petals. I felt my heart leap and I longed to hug that child. I smiled at her; she beamed back and her parents moved her to the other side of them presumably so as not to distract this strange woman from her prayers! When the opening hymn began I realised that I hadn't got a book. No-one handed me one. Did they not realise that I had organised the liturgy for years and often intoned the singing? Who cared about that now?

I found it peculiar just being one of the congregation and knew I would have to accept that because I no longer wore a habit, no one would show me the special respect and deference that went along with the title 'Sister' and the knowledge that a nun was a consecrated person who had given her whole life to God.

After the final hymn, 'Now the Mass Is Ended, Lord', was finished I made my way in the crowd to the back porch and was delighted to recognise Anna, an ex-nun I had met previously on a renewal course run for nuns. She invited me to her house and told me about an organisation known as the Advent Group who helped people who were leaving religious life.

'Why don't you come along? I'm going on Saturday next. We could go together.'

I did and sat in a semi-circle with other men, women and children awaiting the commencement of Mass. Out came the priests, some wearing vestments and others in lay attire. After, when we were having refreshments, I was introduced to the wives and children of the priests who had been officiating and discovered that they had wanted to remain priests while being married and having a family. They seemed to be angry that while the Catholic Church was welcoming married Anglican clergy, many of whom were changing over because they could not accept the woman priests now allowed by the Anglican Church, it was not prepared to tolerate them. It all seemed strange. Priests with wives and children!

'Well, what do you think?' enquired Anna on the front seat of the bus home.

'How long have you been out?'

'Two years this May.'

'Can I ask you for advice? I mean what should I do? Oh — it's — well, how d'you know?'

'You just know. No one can tell you. You just know if it is right for you. Nobody else can make this big decision for you.'

I knew she was right and I was also becoming more aware that the life I had been leading had been meaningless for me for years.

'D'you know,' I said, 'it feels like it did when I discovered that there was no Santa Claus. I laughed and cried all at once because I couldn't believe that I had been fool enough to believe in him for all those years — and I also was stunned to think that my own parents had been telling lies for so long.'

23

Signing Off

Dear God, what's that?
I had my hand up to shade my eyes from the morning sun. Gradually I parted my fingers to see the letter on the floor under my door.
Jesus, what time is it? Oh! It's OK. I'm on holiday. It's mid-term. But who's it from?
Lying on my bed I focused on that envelope. I slid from between the sheets. As I held it I recognised the writing.
Jesus, it's Mother Provincial!
My damp nightie stuck to my back.
I guessed what this letter would be about. I got back into bed, pummelled my pillow, clutched a handful of tissues and used my index finger to cut along the top of the envelope.
It read:

Dear Sister Marion,
You will be aware that you have had more than the recommended time for discerning whether or not you wish to be released from your vows. You must realise

263

that it is in your own interest to make your decision.

Read Article 105 of the Constitutions and of the Regulations and you will see that you are required to write your request to our Holy Father, the Pope, and this is to be sent through me to the Superior General who will forward it to the Vatican.

I have enclosed a few sheets of house-headed paper for this purpose.

If you want to come over and discuss matters, ring and you will be given an appointment.

God Bless
Sister Miriam

In the customary way she had signed herself 'Sister' rather than 'Mother' as a sign of humility.

Sticky stuff clammed my sore eyes. The tissue was too hard to clean my glasses. I held on to the mattress and let myself flop back down under my duvet, letting the letter float to the carpet. Turning my back away from the morning light, I firmly closed my eyes and prayed:

Please, Jesus, help me sleep!

My mind wandered back to those I had known who had left religious life over the years. There was Kathy and Martin. They had fallen in love when they were putting on a production of *Romeo and Juliet* with the sixth formers! Fact stranger than fiction or what? He was a priest and she a fully-fledged nun. The Superior had not succeeded in squashing the scandal because they refused to hide their love for each other and besides it slowly became obvious that Kathy was pregnant and attending the local medical practice while still wearing her religious habit.

Then there had been Marie Black who hailed from Derby and had married the Father Superior of the Fathers of Saint John Xavier. That was another story with a happy ending that had received ample coverage in a few journals.

But what about those two who had left years ago? What were their names? Was it Sister Annette and Sister Evelyn? It had been rumoured that Annette was a brilliant cook and Evelyn had worked in the laundry and they had left and set up home together and had ended up living a ghastly destitute life since Annette had discovered that she was an alcoholic and Evelyn became crippled with arthritis. Had that version of events been spread about to scare off those who were contemplating leaving?

I tossed and turned and eventually got up,

went to the bathroom, came back, cleared a space at my desk and read the letter again. Spots of rain pinged against the window. I went out to the kitchenette, measured four spoons of muesli into my bowl, poured on the milk and went back into my bedroom. It had become cold enough to have the heating on so I sat on the floor with my back to the warming radiator and forced down my breakfast.

Dear Lord, is it better to write straight away? I have made up my mind, haven't I? I couldn't go back, not now. Maybe I should just go over and see the Sisters once more, just casually. Or should I discuss this serious matter with the Mother Provincial? Take up her offer and make an appointment.

But I had done so much talking so often. And I needed to get things sorted while I was on half term rather than wait for an appointment.

I could hear Mrs Poliskie hoovering the porch. I listened until she switched off and went back beyond the door that separated us.

I crept out to run a bath, but the water was tepid so I just dipped myself in and out and got dried and pulled on a track suit my brother had given me.

It was half past eleven. I sat at my desk and took some scrap paper and wondered what was the proper way to address the Pope.

Mary, my Mother, I hate all these formalities.

I thumped the desk.

'To pot with titles and bowing and scraping and rules and regulations! Rules and more rules!'

I suddenly realised I was speaking aloud. I walked about the room.

Isn't it that I'm trying to get away from? Why should I care about all these men in Rome telling us women how to live subservient lives while they swish about in purple robes and please no one but themselves? No, I am not going to comply and use headed paper!

I sat and taking a page of plain white A4 paper wrote:

> *6, Moonshine Avenue*
> *Wimbledon*
> *London SW19 8PR*
> *6th January 1991*

Dear Pope John Paul II,
*   I, Marion Dante, want to be released from the vows I made on August 5th 1965 as a member of the Religious Order of Daughters of Mary Help of Christians (Salesian Sisters) founded by Saint John Bosco . . .*

I couldn't continue. I rummaged in my school bag for my clipboard and some scrap paper and positioned myself on the edge of my bed with the front of my legs against the radiator under the window that looked on to the back garden, still so bleak at this time of year. Would the peony roses and gladioli revive in spite of the bitter winter wind and rain? Would the arms of the copper beech and alder reach out again as the season changed? I folded the page in half down the middle and used one of the blue biros I had acquired from school to draw headings on either side of the divide:

Advantages of leaving:	Disadvantages:
1 Marry the man of my dreams.	1 Alone in old age.
2 Be myself/live my beliefs.	2 Begin again at 46.
3 Stop living a lie.	3 Accept that I've wasted a good chunk of my life.
3 Be rid of community life.	3 Family ties broken/not used to me contacting them.
4 Put an end to the pain.	4 No one to care for me physically and mentally.
5 Have a home and comfort.	5 Be only given £6000 after a lifetime's work.

6 Comparatively young.	6 Past child bearing/have given my best years.
7 No longer have to teach.	7 Not too far off retirement/ not much of a pension.
8 Trained as teacher/degree.	8 CV too Catholic.

Mrs Poliskie was in the garden waving up to me. The rain had stopped. I put my hand up to wave back and remembered I hadn't combed my hair.

Dear Lord, what if I were to go back to the convent and try again?

So I did. Putting on my warm navy-blue mack and making sure I had my travel card I walked down to the station, caught the train straight away and the connecting bus and rang the convent doorbell.

And Maeve answered.

'Come on in! How are you? We're just about to eat. Well timed. True to form, you smelt the stew.'

'Thanks, Maeve. I'm starving. I'm not much use at cooking for myself.'

Once back at the table I was the centre of attention, laughing and joking.

Lord, how could I leave these friends?

We washed up and tidied away and exchanged stories about the children we taught. Then it was time for chapel. I sang as heartily as ever and got sentimental over the psalms and prayers.

'Sister Rita has been begging in the market again and we have a few bits and pieces that might interest you,' Maeve told me as she led the way into a spare room. 'There now, how do you like that skirt and jacket? You need to be fashionable! And there's jewellery here. That ring might fit you. It's better to wear a ring and there is a matching heart-shaped necklace too.'

I began to sob, to cry, to heave with tears. She came near and handed me tissues. 'You needn't go, you know.'

The more kindness she showed me the more I cried and eventually by telling Sister Alice that I wasn't feeling well, Maeve got permission to drive me back to my Wimbledon patch. We parted, with me promising to take care.

I rushed upstairs lest I should meet my landlady. I unlocked my door and saw the letter I had begun.

Jesus, shall I tear it up?

But I knew deep down that I couldn't take such a retrograde step.

So armed with a mug of coffee, I continued what I had begun:

★　★　★

I have tried hard during the three years granted me to consider whether or not I should renew my vows and have come to the conclusion that I find it too difficult to continue living in the convent. I therefore feel that, for the good of my health, I want to be released from the commitment of being a Sister in the Salesian Order.

★ ★ ★

When I put my coffee to my lips, my glasses steamed up and when I removed them the tears flowed. Blowing my nose and mopping my eyes gave me a headache, so I did what I rarely did and swallowed two Nuorofen to dull the pain. This actually made me drowsy and so I lay on my bed and fell asleep.

It was the rain pattering at my window that woke me about an hour later and when I looked at the letter I saw that the writing was shaky and my wet tissues had made it damp. I rewrote it and decided that maybe it might be better to sign off:

Yours respectfully,
Marion Dante

I addressed the envelope to:

His Holiness Pope John II
The Vatican
Roma
ITALIA

24

New Life, New Clothes

All through the week after I had posted my letter I felt that I was stepping on a flimsy surface out in the middle of an immense lake.

Dearest Jesus, I'd love to have faith and believe that if I called out you would do what you did for Peter and come walking on the Sea of Galilee with your arm outstretched ready to comfort me. But as my faith is wavering I would surely sink.

★   ★   ★

I lay in bed the following Saturday morning, unable to even lift my eyelids as snapshots of my past flickered before me. The faded brownish yellow ones showed me when I left home on 25th August 1959. There was my mother, my brothers and sister and me dressed in my smart school navy-blue blazer over a pale blue dress, a velour hat with a shield-shaped badge, white socks and black lace-up shoes. With the red patent Dolcis slip-on shoes hidden under the interlock vest and knickers in my case. The next page of this album had just turned over, showing my mother about to give me half a crown for the taxi to get to Chertsey, when I heard a knock on my bedroom door.

Forcing my eyes open I murmured, 'God, who's that?'

'Sorry! Thought you'd be . . . sorry, it's . . .'

Grabbing my dressing-gown I opened the door.

'Oh . . . em . . . hello. I . . .'

Lord, what's my landlady doing outside my room?

I glanced quickly round to see if her son Mark's door was closed. What if he saw me in this state of undress?

'Look, I'm sorry, I bought some lovely croissants and you can probably smell the coffee. I — well, on a Saturday, especially when the two men are not here, I just take it easy and I wondered if maybe you'd like to join me . . . but, sorry, I'm disturbing you . . .'

'Oh no, no, not at all, Mrs Poliskie.'

'Janeen, I'd like you to call me Janeen.'

'Janeen. Yes, why not? I'll just get dressed — or maybe I'll — well, as you are still in your dressing-gown maybe I'll come down like this?'

I hadn't washed and my faded floral dressing-gown was threadbare, my long blue, brush-nylon nightdress not at all like the skimpy bits visible through Janeen's matching nightie affair. This all seemed so decadent!

Barefoot, I tiptoed behind her downstairs into her sitting room noticing that everything she had, from clothes to upholstery, was of good quality, tasteful and matching — autumn shades and hues on curtains, carpet and even the fine china mug she offered me was gold-rimmed.

'What a beautiful scene! Do you paint?' I pointed to the picture on the long wall facing us.

'That's a print. It's a lesser-known Constable. I fell in love with it years ago. We've got similar tastes perhaps? But, tell me, how are you managing?'

I told her how I travelled to school each day and generally coped with my new life outside the convent but she wanted to know so much.

'I hope you won't mind me asking you but where do you get your clothes, Marion?'

Dear Lord, do I look that strange? How am I supposed to answer?

'Things get handed in for fetes and jumble sales, you know, that kind of thing.' There was a pause. Then I giggled. 'But I do remember the first time a few of us went away on holiday and got dressed up in lay clothes!'

'Lay clothes? What d'you mean?'

'Oh, I mean ordinary clothes — not a habit.'

With the fresh bread and strong coffee aroma I felt relaxed enough to put my feet up on a brown-textured-material footstool. Then I began to tell Janeen how four of us nuns managed our first holiday ever in Worthing.

'Well, maybe I should explain that up until fairly recently we were not allowed to go on holiday because it was believed that every second of our lives had to be spent usefully. The saying *'The Devil finds work for idle hands'* was often quoted or we were reminded of the words of our founder, Saint John Bosco: *'I have promised God that I shall work for my poor boys to my last breath.''* I explained that by the seventies it was becoming acceptable for us to go away for a week to another convent that did not belong to our Order to have a break from our ordinary work. But we had to be able to go to daily Mass, say our prayers and be together in a group in approved accommodation. Four of us in the late thirty to forty age-group had found a guesthouse run by the Sisters of Our Lady of Fatima in a quiet area of Worthing that satisfied these requirements.

'Do you know, I never imagined it was like that for nuns! Poor you!'

Dear Jesus, everything seems so strange! We're doing nothing on a Saturday morning. I'm not even washed and I'm sitting here telling this woman all our secrets.

'You OK? I'm curious but you don't have to tell me if you don't want to.' Janeen reached over to pat my hand.

'No, no! I'm fine.' So I continued with my story. 'One day, on one of our 'holidays', Cecilia, our arty absentminded professor type, quaint Hilary, practical Pat and I arranged to meet on the landing outside our bedrooms after breakfast. We had decided to come out without our habits, wearing whatever outfits we had managed to acquire. My sister had given me a knee-length elasticated beige skirt, a matching blouse and cardigan. That she was two sizes bigger than me meant that I was well covered and modest. My hair had recently been suitably cropped by one of the other nuns.'

Janeen pulled a face.

'Yes, I know! I must have looked awful! Anyway, I arrived out of my room at the same time as Pat who looked very fetching in a blue striped jumpsuit and navy jacket. Her flecked black hair curled round her cherub features. We had to wait a long time before

Hilary emerged wearing a really drab old-fashioned, button-through, dark-brown dress covered over by a long woolly cardigan. All she needed was the pillar-box hat with the feather to remind me of my grandmother! Fortunately, her brunette bun hairstyle lifted her whole appearance and even made her look glamorous. Then we waited for Cecilia. Eventually the door opened and she came out, holding up strands of her hair, saying, 'Has any of you got an elastic band? That's what's kept me. My hair's so wispy!' She had tried to scoop all the bits of hair she possessed into a very high ponytail and to hold it together with a scrap of material like the braiding from around a pocket!'

Janeen laughed, obviously enjoying the story.

'We each struggled to keep back the laughter as we eyed her outfit. There she was in an overall, which she must have taken from the school dinner cupboard! It was bright yellow with a brown check and had grubby white collar and cuffs. What's more, the pop socks she had on finished below the knee and so did not meet the hem she had obviously just let down! Well, we eventually all burst out laughing — which was unkind — but we couldn't help it!'

'What did you do?' chuckled Janeen. 'She

must have looked a sight. I thought you said she was artistic?'

'After a lot of laughter I loaned her my full-length black nun's mack! Then we agreed to try and find a charity shop to see if we could get her something more suitable. We ventured out and found one on the corner of the main street. But we had only been there a few minutes when we were taken aback to hear, 'Sisters, what do you think?' from her as she stuck her head out of the changing room.'

'So?'

'You see, by addressing us with our title 'Sisters' we considered that she had blown our cover immediately and from then on everybody would know we were nuns. So Pat stayed with her and we waited anxiously outside until she eventually joined us wearing a dark green wrap-over skirt and a yellow and green striped top.'

'How did she look?' asked Janeen.

'She looked better than the rest of us! So off we went to the beach.'

'You weren't intending to go in the sea, were you?' asked Janeen.

'But, of course we were! That was to be the highlight of our stay. Up until the Retreat that year we had not been allowed to swim and now we could. But this was a different deal to the empty beaches in Ireland where I used to swim years ago. Worthing pebble beach was crowded and the sun was full out as we approached, each trying to look as though we knew how ordinary people get on with whatever it was people do on a strand. Pat exchanged her sandals for flip-flops and wobbled nonchalantly to a shaded spot near a breaker, put her towel out and sat down. We followed and did the same. Then Pat put another towel over her shoulders and in no time emerged in a swimsuit. I admired her courage and know-how but I was shaking and had suddenly developed goose pimples and the wind blowing through my hair felt very cold and invasive. I missed my veil and yet here I was, about to let my chalky white skin out into the air and let everyone view my entire body shape. Just as I was about to be courageous, I caught sight of Cecilia spreading out her big black, nun's mack over the stones! Pat, on seeing this, got up, stuck her arm through Cecilia's and forced her to walk up and away above the beach with her. We all held our breath until some minutes later a chastened Cecilia arrived back and we, responding to Pat's signalling, moved all our stuff to another part of the beach!'

'Did you eventually get in?'

'Yes, I did after a long time. We must have been there over an hour by the time I managed to take my clothes off bit by bit, trying to adjust to the feel of the air on my body and the stones on my feet, pebbles catching on my toes. And finally braving the coldness and freedom of the sea up to my ankles, to my knees, allowing the waves to wash and spray my bottom, back, arms then shoulders as I went under, froze and then was revived and released in the energy of the sea. But once I jumped and flopped and let go on my back I did not want to leave the embrace of that salty existence. I was like a child again and I could see my mother swimming far out beyond the waves in the Atlantic Ocean. Having just a swimming costume on felt great and I longed for it to go on for ever and ever!'

'D'you know, no-one would ever imagine what it must be like for you to start wearing ordinary clothes after all those years in a habit. I mean, what was the habit like?'

'Janeen, it has changed a good deal over the years!'

'Oh go on, I'm curious, it's not often you get to talk to a real nun. Can I top you up? I'll put another couple of croissants in the microwave. Please?'

How could I refuse when she returned and temptingly allowed the warm smell of the croissants and the fresh brew to entice me? So, replenished and still in my nightwear, seated in a very comfortable sitting room in well-heeled Wimbledon, I began telling my fortyish-something landlady what we nuns wore. There she was looking so delicate and frilly with long dark-brown hair falling loosely down over a slim, bronzed body, her big, open expression curiously soaking up every word of explanation I gave about my very different life. There was only the gentle ticking of a distant clock and birdsong from the well-kept garden that we could almost touch through the opened French doors.

'You don't mind, do you?'

Jesus, I do, but I need friends too and she's so good to me so I'll reply, 'Of course not.'

So it was that I made some attempt to explain how we had started out with home-made underwear and a bib called a *modestino* and all the various veils etc.

'Considering what you wore you were very courageous to take off your clothes and go swimming in Worthing! In fact you must be feeling strange today to be in your nightgear down here with me at nearly eleven o'clock on a Saturday morning!'

I swallowed the remains of my lukewarm coffee. 'Yes, I think I'd better be getting dressed now.'

I left the sitting room to go upstairs, feeling strange but very good about my session with

Janeen. It was the closest I had come yet to life outside the convent. I felt some hope at last about my prospects of living as an 'ordinary' person.

As I reached the landing Janeen shouted, 'The post must have arrived while we were deep in conversation. Here! There's one for you!'

One glance at the writing and I saw straight away that it was from Maeve.

25

Calamity Community

Dear Marion,

Could we meet on Saturday next on platform 14, under the archway near the phones, on Clapham Junction? I can be there by 2.30. Please phone before to confirm. I'm on duty on Thursday. Usual shift: 6 to 10 p.m.

Hope you can manage this.

Be brave. God Bless.
Maeve

Maeve was waiting for me when I arrived. She had to put down her big bag to hug me. I was glad that she was not wearing her habit because this made her less conspicuous when we moved downstairs into a station cafe.

As I took a tray and went to order she whispered, 'Don't bother getting 'eats'.'

I understood what she was up to when I joined her at a corner table and she surreptitiously produced biscuits.

'Where did you say you were going?' I

enquired, knowing that she must have made up some story to be allowed out alone.

'My confessor in Ealing Abbey,' she said, almost forcing a smile. 'How are things?' Then standing up and doing a twirl, she added, 'How do I look?'

Putting on a modelling commentator's voice I said, 'Perfect! The brown in your eyes is enhanced by the golden colours in the dress! Where did you get it? No, don't tell me, you found it in the jumble. Am I right?'

'Thank you!' She inclined her head in a bowing gesture. 'I was frightened, though, that I'd meet any of the schoolchildren in this outfit.'

'Well, it is a bit risky meeting up at the Junction.'

'But it was worth it and I need cheering up. I have missed the laughs and in fact I was giggling, at least I was trying to cheer myself up, coming along here by thinking about the day the man tried to sell Sister Mary Brown the manure!'

'The very thing and her all holy after just coming out of chapel! Well, she would rush to open the door!'

'Ah, but she didn't expect to find a Traveller man there!' Putting on her Kerry accent and acting the part, Maeve began, ''Sister, or is it Reverend, could I interest you in the very best manure for putting on your roses? I'll even shovel it over 'em myself!''

'No, thank you,' I said, mimicking Sister Mary Brown's voice.

'Maybe you'd reconsider that quick 'no' if you were informed of the real bargain I'm offering you, Reverend!'

'The answer is *no* whatever the price,' I said in Sister Mary's stiffest tones.

'And could I ask you why?'

'Because we make our own!'

'And then Sister Mary Brown collapsed in laughter against the wall before returning to the community still listening in silence to the reading of the life of Mother Morano!'

We laughed, but it seemed to me that Maeve's laugh was a little forced, even though it was she who had brought the classic convent anecdote up.

We reminisced for about an hour over the one pot of tea and I wondered when she would unload her worries that afternoon. I was not surprised then when eventually a shade fell over her face and her eyes welled up.

'Would you mind walking up to a little garden up the hill for a bit?' Tiny tears began to trickle.

When we reached the garden, Maeve explained that she was feeling confused and

286

worried, so much so that she was afraid it would affect her health. 'I just feel so very weak,' she whimpered.

After a while it became clear that in spite of being a relatively strong character, Maeve was now experiencing some of the psychological bullying I'd imagined had been peculiar to my own struggle. So when she related an instance in which an Italian nun, Sister Carina, had cornered her in a small office, pointed her finger at her and succeeded in intimidating her by telling her, among other things, that she was disgracing the Sisters by not always wearing her veil and threatening her that she would report this to her superiors, I felt in some way relieved. This was because similar things had happened to me and I recognised her frustration. Besides, having recently returned from Ireland where I had witnessed the gradual updating that was taking place in our Order there, I expected more changes this side of the water.

'Maeve, I have suffered similar treatment. Does it help you to know that?' I stretched my hand out to touch hers. 'I had nearly come to accept that those of us who wanted to make progress have to put up with being accused of being selfish and forgetting the spirit of the Founder. But as time passed I realised that I was not being listened to and I do not agree with any Sister being cowed into submission.'

'Why didn't you tell me this before? I felt so stupid — I've been feeling so guilty!' Her hands were up in the air and she looked as though she was about to smile and cry simultaneously.

'What can I say? I wasn't sure myself. And all that about charity and taking another person's good character away, you know!'

'Estrina isn't happy and maybe she realises that she is too old to leave now. Maybe that is why she takes it out on others.'

'Maeve, shall I tell you when it dawned on me that I was totally obsessed with living my life here on earth so that I would merit a heavenly reward?'

She nodded and I explained how one night in the refectory when the list of the Sisters who had died was being read out, it suddenly hit me that I would actually be dead when my illustrious name came to be read and so not be around to take pride in my success! It was like waiting to hear the kind praise that people only give to those they know, after they are dead and gone!

'So, what you're saying to me is 'Get a life and get out!''

'No! No! Maeve, I can't make decisions for you. All I know is that you need help now and another thing, while you are feeling so weak is not the best time to make drastic changes or big decisions.'

'I can't go on living the way I am. Please help me, Marion, please? If you don't, I think I will end up doing something awful.'

I was very concerned about Maeve as I walked her back down towards the convent and she handed over all the food she had secretly acquired for me and had carried about in her bag all afternoon. When we said goodbye I so much hoped she would find someone who could help her.

For the next week the pile of food I struggled to use before it went off was a constant reminder of Maeve. As I ate bacon with every meal I thirsted for information from the closest thing I'd ever had to a friend.

On the following Wednesday I called in at the convent en route home from school and heard that Maeve was in bed sick. When I went into her room and saw her I felt I had failed her. Her sallow skin looked so wan and weak and her lack-lustre hair clung to her sunken jaws. Her breath smelt, too. I asked her what I could do for her and she said that she had made plans and was determined to get revenge on those who had reduced her to this sad state.

'That sounds bad!'

'Well, I don't care!' were the last words she managed to share with me before Sister Carina looked in on us and smiled.

Dear Jesus, this is typical of this nun! What has made her so two-faced?

Two days later Maeve recovered enough to be sitting waiting for me on a bench near my Wimbledon patch when I returned from school. She came up to my room and sobbed inconsolably and I am sure Janeen must have heard her.

When I questioned Maeve about what had happened she described the anomalies in behaviour I had come to know so well. There would be nothing tangible but a distinct atmosphere giving the place a clinical feel. Sister Carina seemed to generate this and then there would be collusion so that the smiles and exterior signs of courtesy prevailed at the same time as jagged movements and sharp replies.

'I felt so spiteful that I brought you round one of those special *'panatone'*. They'll be wondering how it got eaten up so quickly!' gloated Maeve as she handed me the box in an M&S bag.

26

Retaliation

Maeve hid Sister Carina's stamp collection. She deliberately opened her locker and took all the foreign stamps that she had been collecting for years and hid them in a cupboard that was rarely used. She even said that she had been sorely tempted to trade them in a Stamp Collectors Shop in the High Street. I expect she was thinking that the money she'd get would come in useful.

'Well, no Sister is supposed to have anything of her own. The Rule says so and she's lectured us on this often enough.'

'Good job you didn't sell them because she would certainly have recognised her stamps in the shop especially if they had been put in the window! You would have been in serious trouble then!'

'Part of me wishes I had done just that. You see, she wouldn't have been able to report her loss simply because she is fully aware that according to the Holy Rule she should have 'Freed herself of the desire to possess'! Ah, this is only the beginning of the punishment I intend to mete out to Sister Carina! OK, I won't go overboard but as they say 'Watch this space'!'

Maeve had managed to sneak out again to visit me in my flat.

This time Janeen brought us up apple strudel and cream because she said that we cheered her up by laughing so much. I had just managed to hide the nougat from Turin, known to the Italians as 'Terroni', that Maeve had brought me over from the convent, as Janeen knocked at my door.

When Janeen left we sat on the floor and I continued telling Maeve about an article I had spotted in the paper about George Harrison. It was that which led us on to discussing the Beatles and how we felt we had missed out on having pop-star idols.

'You won't believe this but once when my brother Des came to visit me he asked me if I had seen the Beatles. I looked down on the ground and replied, 'No, we keep this place very tidy. I don't think you'd find any beetles here!''

'Just think, George lives in the house where we did our noviciate from '63 to 65! Do you think Sister Maria Teresa Pranzo haunts him?' laughed Maeve.

'Don't talk to me about that woman! It was she who made me eat an egg for breakfast after I had been out in my chicken veil and apron with Sister Beatricia killing chickens! I felt sick!'

'Chicken veil?'

'Yes, we had special 'chicken clothes' which we wore for the operation — chasing and grabbing the chicken, wringing its neck and then plucking and cleaning it out. Did you never have to do that job?'

'No, thank God!'

'You missed out. On that occasion one hen had got away with its head half off!'

'Oh that's disgusting! That's the pits! Animal rights would have you up for cruelty! The poor creature!'

'What about poor me having to do it?'

'Well, I hope you finished her off properly!'

'Sister Beatricia did. I was on that job for half my noviciate and on the sacristy for the rest of the time. Talk about contrast!'

'But — the egg you had to eat — didn't you say anything?'

'It was Retreat day so I wasn't even permitted to talk — I tried to refuse, shaking my head and so on, but she wasn't taking no for an answer! And anyway you know the saying we had that 'A good appetite — ''.

' 'Is a sign of a good vocation!' '

When I came downstairs to wave Maeve off, Janeen just happened to be saying farewell to a Mr Hotham who asked Maeve if she wanted a lift.

Thinking nothing of the incident I waved as the Merc drove off. I was just about to move upstairs when Janeen asked me how often I had gone on spiritual retreats and how helpful I had found them. It transpired that she was considering the one being promoted by the Jesuits up in our parish.

'We made retreats on the first Saturday of each month and for eight days annually. Our big retreat takes place late July into August.'

'Any particular reason for the date?'

'Yes, that is the period when the novena to Our Lady of the Snows takes place. Her feast day is 5th August.'

'Snow in August?' asked Janeen, raising an eyebrow.

'Yes, legend has it that Our Lady indicated in a dream to a wealthy Roman couple that she wanted a church built in her honour and the site for this church would be covered with snow. So on a hot, sultry morning on 5th August, Esquiline Hill in Rome was covered with snow. All Rome proclaimed the summer snows a miracle, and a church to honour Mary was built on the hill in 358 A.D.'

'I like that!' said Janeen.

'It's also the anniversary of my becoming a Bride of Christ and making my vows of

Poverty, Chastity and Obedience.' My eyes filled up and I took out a tissue. 'It should be my silver jubilee this year.'

Janeen put her hand over her mouth and bending towards me apologised, 'Marion, I'm sorry. I didn't think. This must all be very upsetting for you.'

Recovering, I stammered, 'No, it's all right, I'd rather talk about it. Shall I tell you what it is like?'

'Only if you want to.'

Janeen's eyes were like satellite dishes sensitive to every probe as I described those early days.

'Marion, you have been through a lot. Come in with me and have a glass of wine before you go upstairs and have nightmares tonight!'

27

Only Daughter

Who was this Mr Hotham who gave Maeve a lift back to Clapham convent from my bed-sit in Wimbledon?

Mr John and Mrs Ann Hotham celebrated the birth of their daughter on 22nd July 1969, the day after the three men first walked from Apollo 11 on the moon. So they called her Paula in the hope that she would launch them off into a happy married life. Their son John was born in 1963, the year that another John, President Kennedy, was assassinated. That completed their family.

In 1991, by the age of twenty-two, Paula had graduated from Oxford, converted to Catholicism and become a nun in our Salesian Sisters Order. Her parents had threatened to disinherit her if she persisted in this lifestyle. Her mother refused to have anything more to do with her but her father drove up to the convent in Henley where she was a novice on most visiting Sundays and she was allowed to meet him at the gate and often persuaded him to chat to her in the gatehouse lodge. It was rumoured that he accepted tea and biscuits, maybe in the hope of winning her over so that she would see sense and return home with him before she made her vows. She refused to believe him when he told her that her mother was ill and neither did he manage to trap her by telling her that he would change his Will in favour of her brother John if she became a nun. She instead informed him that by her vow of poverty she would be renouncing all her worldly wealth on her profession day.

Paula's father was a governor in the school where my landlady's husband taught. We discovered this when Maeve and I were invited to an end-of-term evening buffet and drinks hosted by landlords Mr Mark and Mrs Janeen Poliskie.

We had cut each other's hair and procured suitable outfits from what was handed in to be sold to boost convent coffers. We even experimented with a little make-up to complete our camouflage.

Janeen invited Maeve after she had come up to console her when she heard her crying a few nights previously. Although Maeve had gone home that night protesting, 'I detest being felt sorry for!' she had willingly accepted Janeen's invitation to this 'do'. She was to regret this, though, when in spite of turning up in a slimming black and white number, hoping to disguise her real identity, Janeen had introduced her to the guests using her title 'Sister Maeve'.

Mr Hotham latched on to Maeve before she realised that his daughter Paula was in her community. After the meal when I accompanied her to Wimbledon Station she told me that a Mr Hotham had plied her with questions about why I was leaving the convent and why she was not wearing her habit.

'I hope you didn't give away too much, Maeve.'

'Why?'

'You didn't find out who he is then?'

'Glory, just who was I talking to, Marion?'

'Sister Paula's father.'

'God no!'

'Afraid so, Maeve. Mr Hotham has been one of the governors of St Christopher's Grammar since his two children Paula and John went there years back. I'd have warned you but I only found that out myself this evening.'

'All I need now is for it to get back to Sister Carina that I have been with you instead of seeing my spiritual director over in Ealing tonight! It's bad enough having to change in the garage without this pressure!'

As I waved Maeve off that evening she probably did not realise that I was also concerned about what would happen to Paula as a result of what Maeve had told him about community life in Clapham.

It was over a week later that I received a little thank-you note from Maeve saying that Sister Carina was not so bad after all and enquiring why I had not called in to see them in Clapham recently. So the following Monday I arrived for supper with the Sisters.

The Sister Cook who had recently joined the community had not catered for our tastes or prepared the Italian-style meal we enjoyed. She looked very downcast, still dressed in the black outdated version of the habit. I knew she had repeatedly asked if she would be permitted to study and acquire sufficient exams to qualify her to go to teacher-training college, but different superiors had consistently refused her over the years. That night she only replied when spoken to and was not present at recreation when we socialised. When I enquired about her, I was informed that she was still settling in and had retired early.

Sister Carina sat next to me offering to replenish my wine glass. 'You look as though you could do with a well-deserved rest — after all, you've had a hard year's teaching,' she said. Then, leaning over in her armchair, and almost whispering, she added, 'Sister Paula was telling me that her father met you when he was at your place, or rather, the house where you rent a bed-sit, for a similar end-of-term celebration. Small world, eh?'

I managed to smile, turn slightly and reach out for a vol-au-vent from a passing tray while wondering how much Sister Carina knew. It was imperative to find out from Maeve what had happened that night she had arrived after the 'do' but I couldn't get her on her own. In desperation, while I was in the bathroom, I wrote her a note asking her to meet me, and I slipped it into her hand as I left.

I waited for over forty minutes the following day outside Saint Anne's Church for Maeve to arrive. While I resented maintaining so much contact with the Sisters in the time I had been given to assess if it would be better for me to leave religious life, I had become protective towards Maeve and concerned what lengths she might be led to, were she to become too frustrated or thwarted.

'Hello, Sister Marion! It's a long time since we saw you!' shouted a girl and then I remembered that the parish catechists prepared the children for their Confirmation at the church at this time.

When Maeve eventually appeared she was with two Sisters from the Windlesham community. I was delighted to see these two genuinely good souls. The former was as thin as a lampstand and seemed to maintain her size by cooking excellent meals for others. I knew the other to be a mature well-balanced and self-educated Mayo woman. As a team they worked well together and maintained a sense of wellbeing and sanity in any community. They were a real asset to live with because you could say anything you wished to the Mayo woman and know it would remain safe with her and, if you were just tired, the other one would see you got to bed and were well nourished while you were there. This was in spite of the fact that it was commonly held that tiredness had to be overcome and that bed was only resorted to in times of illness when one certainly did not require feeding.

'It's great to see you, Marion! *Aon scéal?*' she asked — the Irish for 'Any news?'

'Well now, how long have you got?' I laughed.

'Is that how it is?'

With that, they left Maeve and me alone. We moved over to a bench and I told Maeve what Sister Carina said to me about Sister Paula's father speaking to me.

'Gee! Does Paula know?'

'That I don't know. Has Estrina said anything to you? Does she know you were there? What did you say to her when you arrived home that night?'

'That's it, you see. I was a little tipsy and she gave me more and I don't drink as you know — we only have it on big feast days and for medicinal reasons. I sang the Abbot's praises.' Abbot Rushden was the spiritual director she'd been supposed to be seeing that night. 'As I was supposed to be getting personal guidance I knew she couldn't question me. I didn't mention the lift home.'

'Did you have any traces of make-up on you that night? Might you have given the game away on yourself?'

'I don't know. I wasn't fully compos mentis. But how did Estrina know Paula's father was there?'

'The only thing I can think of is that Mrs Poliskie may have said something to Sister Economer in a letter of acknowledgement for payment of my rent. I mean, she could have innocently given the game away.'

Glum Sister Cook passed us then and we fell silent, then our conversation died a natural death when the Angelus Bell summoned the community to church and we parted company once more.

28

Sisters

Before I put the key in the door of 50 Moonshine Road, I could hear the phone ringing. I didn't hurry because Mrs Poliskie had said that she would prefer that I did not receive calls on what was essentially their family phone. The ringing stopped as I reached for a letter left for me on the side table and climbed upstairs. I had barely eased my sweaty feet out of my bargain shoes when the phone rang again. I opened my door and listened. Everything was silent and there were no lights on beyond the Poliskie's door. I recalled that the car was not outside the house. Maybe I should just take a message?

'Hello, this is Sist — Marion Dante speaking. May I help you?'

'Sister Marion, it's Paula. I'm so glad it's you. I hope you don't mind.'

'Paula, you're lucky I'm alone in the house. I'm not supposed to get phone calls. How are you?'

'Oh dear! I wanted to talk to you. Is that OK? I'd planned to leave school now and get to your place in about forty minutes' time? I promise I won't stay too long. I can't anyway because I told Sister Superior that I only need to check some information here for tomorrow's lesson, so she'll be expecting me home.'

'I'll have a cuppa ready for you. You're more than welcome. It's just that the landlady wants to reserve the phone for family use. No, anything to help. I'll be expecting you around five. Give three short rings and I'll open up myself. You know how to find me, do you?'

'You sure?'

'Yes, 'course I am.'

'I have an *A to Z*. It looks straightforward. Thanks.'

Luckily my brother Des had given me a packet of biscuits the previous Sunday when I visited him and I ran into the bathroom to check that my milk was still fresh in a bowl of cool water under the bath and the mug Maeve brought me last time she came was next to the kettle.

Dear Lord, I can't seem to settle down and prepare my schoolwork while I'm wondering whether I should tell Paula that I suspect her father is following her. Maybe I was jumping to conclusions because he had only quizzed Maeve after the 'do' and then been at Euston

Station when we returned from Birmingham. But then, what was Sister Carina hinting at when she let me know that she was aware that he had been in my place?

Three sharp rings roused me and I sped down to welcome Paula. No curls this time. She was 'flying the flag' with the full regalia of the new grey habit. I should have guessed that as a fervent newly professed Sister and a recent convert to Catholicism this was only to be expected. But I wondered what the neighbours would be thinking about a visiting nun. Some of them might have already been questioning why a woman in her forties living in this area carried her washing to the laundrette each week. Would they surmise that I was from the convent too?

When we each had a drink and were seated, me on the bed and Paula upright in my armchair, she carefully positioned her mug on the tray on the floor and started, 'I've been accepted for Kingfisher House and I wanted to check out a few details with you before I decide if it is right for me. Do you mind?'

Kingfisher House! She must be too scrupulous or on the verge of a breakdown — at any rate showing signs of a mental state which the superiors recognised as needing expert help.

'As it is top secret I can only discuss it with Sister Superior,' Paula was continuing, 'and she is making her visitations in Scotland this month. Besides, I'd rather hear from you because, having been there, you know first hand.'

I straightened up, hoping she would not probe too deeply. I took a deep breath but she continued before I could say anything.

'John is to be my psychotherapist and, you see, he is a psychiatrist. Why am I being allocated to him? I do not have mental problems. I mean, no more than half the population!'

'Paula, Jerry is better than John!' I half-laughed, Jerry being my own one-to-one therapist. 'No, seriously you are very fortunate to be allocated to him. As for being mad, that is what is feared by almost everyone who agrees to go to Kingfisher House but as the Sister who runs the place says, 'People who question their own sanity need have no fears in that regard'. No, I was helped by the excellent team of therapists there and so were many other people.'

'But you are out here in a bed-sit, starting life again after years of living for the glory of God and working for the evangelisation of the young. That can't be right, can it?'

'It's hard to explain why I'm living here. It

is a time of decision-making for me. Lots of nuns and priests who have been through Kingfisher House are still faithful to their vocations. Don't worry about me — just take this opportunity to see what's right for you. I came to realise that I could still work for young people without being a nun. That was part of my personal journey and it is not easy to explain.' My nerve-endings twinged remembering the painful scrutiny I had encountered in intensive psychotherapy. Trembling inside and pursing my dry lips, I swallowed and continued. 'However, I have to explain to you that the follow-up care after you leave Kingfisher House is not in place. Neither our Order nor the folks up in Kingfisher House seem to have any idea of what it is like to be released from a period of concentrated therapy back into the real world.'

Paula sipped her coffee, let her eyes wander around my room before wrapping her fingers round her warm mug and gently observing, 'You see, what worries me is that I will lose my vocation in Kingfisher House and end up dependent on my parents. My father would love that.'

Although I had observed over the years that others who had converted to Catholicism and immediately embraced religious life often left later, I tried to assure Paula that if she really had a calling to religious life she need have no fear. I wondered though if there were more fundamental problems that she was frightened to face in her life and so, in an effort to lighten both of our spirits, I steered the conversation to what I hoped was an amusing topic.

'How is Sister Catherine Mac Innes? Does she ever talk about the old days when she was an aspirant? Only I was thinking about her today when a girl in front of me on the bus had a tassel on her beret.'

'That must be St Joseph's in Clapham Common. They wear the navy-blue old-fashioned kind of beret with shades of blue tassels attached to a button right in the middle.'

'Well, I don't know, but when I was an aspirant those of us who had joined up still young enough to be going to school had to wear the St John Bosco uniform each day and then return to the convent after school and change into our black dress.'

Paula pinged her fingernail against her mug. 'So, what's the connection?'

'The beret with the tassel — we had them too,' I said in the hope of making her smile. 'Well, one summer's night, Sister Maria Teresa Pranzo — '

'Marion, I hope you don't mind but I need

to get back to be in time for supper.'

'Sorry, but of course you do. You must be tired after school too.'

We both stood and I accompanied her downstairs and out on to the street, embarrassed that my reminiscing had driven her away.

I wondered though why the Superiors saw fit to send Paula to Kingfisher House. No doubt she seemed anxious and a little emotional but maybe she was worried over her parents' reaction to her quick conversion and then becoming a nun so rapidly. Her father might have been genuinely concerned for her well-being. I did feel sorry for him. Would counselling have sorted her problems? Paula was certainly intelligent and different. I remembered one Christmas when she called down the table in her very posh English accent: 'Would someone please pass me the cranberry?' She was still trying to live this down each time one of us recalled this incident.

Once back upstairs, in order to dismiss my fearful feelings, I turned on the television in my head and tried to recapture the incident about the beret. This succeeded in changing my mood as, alone in my kitchenette, I peeled my potatoes, chopped carrots and grilled a chop.

I could visualise our Sister Superior, standing out on the doorstep of the redbrick house that was our *aspirantade* with twenty of us in a semicircle facing her. It was dusk and as we came to the end of our customary singing of a hymn she straightened her veil and the wide sleeves of her habit. It was all very solemn and serious as we waited for her words of wisdom. That night she looked sad and, pointing up at the aeroplanes, she began to lament the fact that because Mother General had become ill she had been deprived of going to Italy and instead had been sent on a visitation to Liverpool. One of the Sisters, a Liverpudlian, shouted out a quotation from a play she was putting on with her class, *'Oh, what a catastrophe!'* in response to this. It was the way she said it, her face contorted and funny!

Smiling to myself on reliving this happening, I turned over my chop. I heard a key turning in the front door and surmised that Mrs Poliskie must be back.

Present reality again suspended, I had to stop myself laughing aloud as I recalled everyone giggling even when we were reprimanded and how, to crown it all, as we filed into chapel and most of us were kneeling in our pews, Catherine appeared around the corner in her black aspirant's dress but wearing one of the school berets with the tassel, instead of her black net aspirant's veil. She must have mislaid her veil and in desperation to have something to cover her head grabbed a blue school beret with a blue and pink tassel from the coat rail on her way. This mismatch of half-aspirant and half-schoolgirl together with her guilty look made her look hilariously funny. We all howled. Even the professed Sisters, who were already kneeling at the back of the chapel waiting for us to join them in saying night prayers, began to snigger. But I recollected that it was only the aspirants who were marched out and admonished and, even when we returned, a sudden snort erupted and a series of snivels and other strange guttural noises continued throughout the prayers and right up into Great Silence supposed to be observed in the dormitory.

But as I carried my tray into my room now I knew fears that made my insides tremble; the remorseless recall of constant self-scrutiny I tried to block was back again. My time in Kingfisher House had left me feeling vulnerable. Had the twelve months of residential psychotherapy cracked or cured me? It certainly was intense and relentless and had left its scars. I was already becoming aware that I, who had always had inclinations to question, pierce, prod into everything, was now too analytical for my own good.

Paula's visit had disturbed me. I had to prepare for school and, being conscientious, I disciplined myself to go through this routine, but all the time I was suppressing the twitches and spasms inside, and my watery eyes meant I had to keep refocusing. Eventually I succumbed and, dropping my clothes over the chair and my nightie over my sagging shoulders, I crumpled into bed. However, I turned over on my side and was just falling off to sleep when I was roused by the sound of keys being turned in the front door. I reached for my torch. Ten o'clock. That must be Mark going to bed. My mind was active again and I could not stop worrying over how I was going to adapt to this new life I seemed to be straying into.

29

The Pope's Answer

Well, the Pope didn't see fit to answer me himself. Nor did he bother to talk me out of my decision to leave.

But an answer did come dated 20th May 1991, only five months after I had given my letter to Mother Provincial to forward to Rome.

Headed *Congregatio Pro Institutis Vitae Consecratae et Societatibus Vitae Apostolicae*, and entirely in Latin, it opened with an extract from Mother Provincial's letter to the Pope about my case:

Most Holy Father

Sister Marion Dante, a perpetually professed member of the Congregation of the Daughters of Mary Help of Christians of this city, begs your Holiness for the indult allowing her to leave the Institute so that she may freely and lawfully return to the secular state in view of the motives set forth . . .

It then continued:

The Congregation for Institutes of Consecrated Life and Societies of Apostolic Life, having given careful attention to the considerations set forth, has given a favourable response to the request so that the suppliant, having laid aside the external form of the religious habit, remains separated from her Institute.

In addition, let the regulation contained in Canon 702, 1 and 2, regarding fair and evangelical charity be observed.

This present rescript, unless refused by the suppliant in the act of its notification, by the law itself, carries with it dispensation from the vows and from all obligations arising from the Profession.

Not withstanding anything to the contrary.

Given at Rome, 29th May 1991

30

Stacking Pennies

'Sorry, Marion, but you'll have to move out.'

'Oh! Really?'

'Don't look so frightened. You probably don't remember but that's what we agreed.'

I didn't remember.

Janeen sat down on the bottom stair step and signalled me to join her. 'If needs be, I'll help you to find somewhere but this form has to be filled in and I am required to declare who's living in my house. I've kept you on as a paying guest but if you stay any longer you'll become a lodger and I'll have to tell the Council and charge you a proper rent. If I don't comply, you would be staying here illegally.'

I had been in Moonshine Road five months when Janeen showed me the Electoral Register form. I understood nothing about this kind of accountability having never filled out such a form in my life.

She hugged me and I blinked back my tears until I closed the door of my room and slid down the back of it and ended slumped on the floor.

Jesus, what am I to do? I've barely got used to my routine and now I have to start all over again. Mary, my Mother, why do I feel so sad?

I levered myself up, pulled my chair next to the window and stared out into the garden. I had begun making piles of the pennies I had managed to save on the window ledge.

Queen of Heaven, I've to learn so many things! How to get a travel pass and find out about zones and timetables. My eyes become sticky and it's not easy to focus. And all the waiting about and the shopping — that's so hard. I struggle to fathom the best way to keep my bread and milk from going off and now I've to look for somewhere to live. I'd just love a little home of my own. What was that poem by Pádraic Colum that Mum used to recite? 'O, To Have A Little House!' How did it go? Something about 'sure of a bed' and a 'ticking clock' and 'speckled and white shining delph' . . .

★ ★ ★

My daily routine was to get up at six, catch the bus to Wimbledon Station, change to the Victoria line train at Clapham Junction, go

316

two stops and arrive at school by 8:30. I was careful not to become friendly enough to have to tell anyone that I was a nun in camouflage.

'You're even earlier today or do you love it so much that you slept here last night?'

'No, John, I came in to root through these Wandsworth Accommodation Lists for Teachers.'

'Funny that. I don't usually read them but the ad for a flat in Putney caught my eye and as the place is round the corner from me I thoroughly recommend the area. Grab it quick or it will be gone.'

'Thanks!'

'Go on then. Out to the office and use the phone now.'

I did and got an appointment to meet a retired head teacher and his wife after school that evening. John gave me a lift and the couple seemed delighted that I was old enough not to want to go out every night!

Jesus, you're looking after me. John's a good man and that flat has two rooms and a shared bathroom on the top of a lovely three-storey house in leafy Putney. I don't like sharing a bathroom but the other young lodger looks shy and the landlady says he's up and out even earlier than me in the morning. Besides, if I wash at night, as the toilet is separate, *I might never bump into him.*

That very evening after school another teacher, the school Deputy, called out to me as I was leaving to catch my train.

'Marion, would you like a lift? I go your way most evenings.'

Oh God, how can I refuse? Thank goodness, now that I'm about to move, I'll be going in a different direction and so won't have to tell her much about myself.

The car was big and she smiled her welcome.

'Look, before we drive off I want you to know that . . . well, because of my trusted position in the school, as Deputy, I know more about you than perhaps you realise.' She reached out and patted my praying hands.

Jesus, it's out! Everybody knows everything about me!

'Don't look so worried. What I know is confidential and I'm only telling you this because a long time ago I trained to be a nun and will never forget how hard it was when I left.'

'Oh Mrs Hughes, I . . . '

'I'm Pat and I would like to help you, only though if that is OK with you. No-one need know your secret and I promise I'll say no more if that's what you prefer.'

My journey home seemed very short that night. Pat asked me questions like how I was coping with my new life and where I got my clothes. It was she who approached the subject of my eventually having a house of my own.

Dear Lord, how does she know my worries and my dreams? In some strange way she seems part of me. It's as though I've known her all my life. Thank you.

Two nights later Sister Rita helped me move to Putney and I began thinking seriously about having a place of my own.

'Mortgage is like gauging how long you're going to live, isn't it?' I said to her.

'How do you mean? Oh, OK — 'morte' — Italian for 'death' — so when you take out a mortgage you're setting it up for as long as you think you will live. I get you.'

'There's no harm done in going into lots of Estate Agents and learning all about buying a house,' Pat Hughes advised when I saw her again. 'Ask questions and listen. Give them lots of scenarios and see what they come up with.'

No matter what way I did my sums I soon realised that no matter how long I might live I'd never be able to save enough to get a mortgage on a London property. So I began applying for teaching jobs outside London. I tried private schools in the hope that I might get 'live in' situations.

I showed my CV and application forms to Pat and she said what I was thinking, 'You're too Catholic for anything other than Catholic schools. Why don't you use these connections to your advantage?'

'Do you know, that's what I've been thinking. I used to teach in Farnborough — the Head has changed but maybe that would work. Great!'

I wrote and the Head phoned me back to tell me that the First Holy Communion class teacher was off to have a baby and he was searching for someone to replace her. Moreover, he had checked me out on the school records and on the strength of my references he was prepared to interview me the following week together with two others who had been short-listed.

'Do you happen to know Marie McGuinness?' he asked.

'She that hails from Ballyferriter?'

'Why, yes, that's where she comes from! Well, she's on the staff. Shall I tell her you're applying?'

★ ★ ★

'Sorry! Sorry! I'm so sorry. What with these sunglasses I can't see!'

320

I had fallen into a crowded five-fifteen train from Clapham Junction to Farnborough Main on the following Friday. Landing on the floor with my legs in the air and minus my glasses. I had tried to plonk myself on a seat that didn't exist! Of course the great British public with their stiff upper lip ignored me. Luckily there was a Celt among them to help me up and ask me if I was OK.

When I told him (and the rest of the folk in the carriage who were pretending not to listen) that I was house-hunting, he offered this advice: 'The upper crust live in Fleet and if you can afford it you could join them. The Paras inhabit Farnborough so avoid them — if you want to opt out of the military set keep to Frimley.'

Most weekends I did my house-hunting from Marie McGuinness's house. It was she who made sure I looked my best for my teaching job interview. They celebrated with me too when I was successful.

Pat and her husband spent many a weekend going round with me to Estate Agents. I found it very difficult to decide and was so anxious when we were being shown around various houses. I couldn't concentrate, to say nothing of deciding which house to settle for.

Lord God, for so many years I've not had

to decide whether I prefer tea to coffee so no wonder I find deciding about mortgaging a house so very difficult.

A Salesian priest put me in contact with a young man who rented me a room in his house in Reading Road while I was house-hunting. I lived there for almost a year.

Pat was with me when I revisited 50 Buckingham Way. She had looked at many houses with me and provided me with a heater and various household items like cutlery while I was living in the one room and searching for a home.

While we were chatting with the lady of the house we could see that she had positioned a playpen to cover a recent coffee stain on the carpet. Nonetheless, we had ticked off seven of the ten things we had listed as being essential for a purchase. We said goodbye and drove away from the house.

'Well?' asked Pat. 'You seem happy — are you? It's going to be your home so it's your choice. It's you who must be satisfied.'

'It's got so many things going for it. I do like it but I'm so very frightened. I want you to take over now. I'm too shaky inside.'

I put my head in my hands which became very sweaty and the tears flowed. Pat put her arms around me and encouraged me to let it all out.

Once she had driven to a café and we settled ourselves with coffees I showed her something I had come across among my papers. It was a list I made of all that I possessed two months before I left the Order:

<u>What I possess</u>   <u>7th May 1991</u>

Tray — new £7.99
1 blue mug
2nd hand kettle
Duvet (2nd hand)
2 pillows & pillowcases (given)
Guitar
Hoover (2nd hand from my sister)
Radio small (3 way)
Tape recorder (cheap)
Tapes 10
Sheets (2 pairs 2nd hand)
Towels (2 sets 2nd hand)
Camera (110 type)
Small plastic alarm-clock
Bedside lamp from my brother
Cases 2
Vases 2
Bible
Divine Office bk (big and small)
Dictionary (paperback)
A to Z streetfinder
Photograph albums 6

Teddy bears (6, various sizes)
Typewriter Brother AX-110
Song books 6
Descant recorder
Ceramics made by me
Electrical lead, 2 plugs, extension lead
Bags (4, various sizes)
Stationery, pencils, pens, rubbers, sello-
tape
Plants (yucca and smaller)
Basin, plastic bucket, potato peeler, can
opener
Hair-dryer, curling tongs,
Make-up, surgical spirits, baby lotion
etc.

Clothes:
All my clothes with the exception of 3
blouses have been given to me. Most of
them were donated by my sister Pat and
my brother Des. The nuns did give me
some years ago.
I have 5 pairs of shoes, a pair of boots
which I bought in Dublin 3 years ago, 2
pairs of trainers and 2 pairs of slippers,
together with tights and socks.

'Well?' I asked Pat. 'Is that not pathetic
after a lifetime's work?'
'Marion, that's why you must go for this

house and begin your new life! You know that no house will have absolutely everything you dreamed of. I think this house is ideal for you. You've taken giant steps in setting up your mortgage and buying your little Rover. You've said you like it so why not go ahead?'

I did and with Pat's help again a week later spent over two thousand pounds in one day buying a fridge, a washing machine and a bed. I treasured Pat's friendship and support. She was a wonderful and generous friend.

31

Cancer

I got the keys for my house after school on Friday at the end of March 1995. Marie McGuinness lent me an armchair that unfolded into a bed and some curtains that I couldn't put up because the previous owners had removed all the fittings.

Earlier that day my new Head Teacher advised me to enlist with a doctor. I did and made an appointment for Maundy Thursday.

Nurse Cox said, 'I see you're fifty so we'd better give you a thorough going over — so if you'd like to pop up there on the bed I'll check your breasts.'

Dear God, what does she mean? I never look at myself so why should I let her? Maybe it's better her than a man doctor? Perhaps normal women just accept this. Better not to make a fuss. 'Tis all so embarrassing!

This I prayed but I said, 'OK but I couldn't be fitter.'

'Can't take chances so if you don't mind . . . won't take long . . . '

Dear Jesus, I wish she would leave me

alone. *All the times I had been told to cover myself! Couldn't she get on with looking after the sick? Why did people keep searching for illness?*

I closed my eyes and let her get on with pressing down my breasts. She did them once and then she did them again.

Then this cheerful, chirpy nurse mumbled something, covered me up as though I was a corpse, patted me and said, 'I don't want to worry you but I can feel three lumps so if you stay there I'm going to check with a doctor.'

She left the room. I kept my eyes closed. A shiver went down my body and I prayed.

Lord Jesus, I'm going to die. Tomorrow is Good Friday.

Ages passed.

The nurse returned to say, 'Dr Yates wants to see you tonight. Can you return at five?'

Can I return? Can I get down from this bed? I'm shaking all over.

'Yes.'

She must have noticed my bewilderment. 'Look, I'm just making sure. I'm only a nurse and you could be perfectly all right but we need to be sure. Of course you're worried but isn't it better to be sure? Try to keep calm. It's not long to wait and you'll know more. All right?'

Tears came. She put her arms round me.

Why was she so kind?

I had that Good Friday feeling: '*The sun stopped shining and darkness covered the whole country and then the curtain hanging in the Temple was torn in two. Jesus cried out in a loud voice: 'Father! Into your hands I commend my spirit!' He said this and died.*' (Luke 23 44–46).

So what if I didn't have furniture in my house! What use was anything if I were going to die?

It was three o'clock. I walked home. I felt mummified. I'd never seen Dr Yates before. When I returned to the surgery I no longer cared that it was a man examining me.

I got down from the bed.

He looked straight at me and asked, 'Have you come on your own?'

I nodded.

He said, 'Yes, you have three lumps. It won't do you any good worrying unduly. Lots of women have lumps and more often than not they turn out to be benign. I'm going to write to the hospital now but because we're coming up to Easter you won't hear from anybody before Tuesday at the earliest.'

I must have walked home. I phoned my sister, mother and my friends. Everybody said the same: 'That's frightening but it might be nothing. Most times it is.'

I went to the Holy Week Services in the Parish Church, but I could only see lumps and think about my imminent death. I phoned the hospital to ask for help but I was told that there was no one there to speak to until after the Easter break. I got angry and demanded to speak to a nurse who listened to my fears and said she couldn't do anything else until we knew what we were dealing with. She gave me lots of phone numbers and I rang them all and cried and howled. I didn't go out that weekend. It dragged past. All I could do was wait until I could phone the hospital again on the Tuesday, then I was told that I would be seen as soon as possible. No one came to visit. No one took me out. I couldn't cry any more.

On the Thursday the hospital phoned to say I had an appointment with a Mr Amery on the following Monday. Thankfully, I was then appointed a Macmillan nurse (these are cancer-care nurses and are a registered charity). I trembled and perspired into my clean underwear in the waiting room. Mr Amery said much the same as the others had said except he added, 'Given your previous good health, if they would allow me I'd take the chance of putting a needle in now and dispersing the lumps. But we have to go through the process and do all the tests.'

I had the tests and went to school and taught my seven-year-olds. People kept talking about things that were going to happen in a week or a month. I had no future. I wondered what they'd say about me when I was dead.

'We didn't really know her — only here barely a year. Looked all right.' Was that what they'd say?

A week later I was told that one of my lumps, that was the size of a golf ball, could be cancerous.

God Almighty, I haven't done anything wrong! I've eaten all the right foods, exercised and been a nun all my life. I've never been in any relationship or had sex!

I said something like this to the doctor and merited this reply: 'Even the Pope can get cancer, you know!'

I was admitted for a lumpectomy. I had to get up early and eat nothing. It was seven thirty in the morning. I walked down to the hospital. There was another woman opposite me. A man, who was most likely her husband, had his hand in hers. Every time the receptionist spoke they looked at each other. I looked at them and they looked back at me. The last time I had been in hospital was when I fell over and had a fractured skull. I was ten and I was in Barrington's Hospital, Limerick.

What happens next? Probably have to undress. What could be worse than exposing my breasts? They called them 'boobs'! How common? Vulgar!

'Mrs Dante?'

Mrs! Why do they think I'm married? Why would I be alone if I was?

I was asked countless questions, mostly the same ones over and over again. I filled in and signed forms and went to the toilet lots of times.

Supposing they cut into the wrong breast? Better write a note to Dr Amery. I'll do that.

The lump is in my left breast.

I trust you. Really I do.

Marion Dante

The man who came to wheel me down laughed at this but told me he'd make sure it was on top of me when I was wheeled in.

The red plastic band on my wrist was to make sure I was not given penicillin. I thought of how my allergy was discovered when I was teaching in Farnborough before I went to college. I caught the flu and the doctor prescribed penicillin which brought me out in a very red rash. However, I was sent back to school before the rash disappeared because I was not deemed to be sick! In any case as I was wearing the old habit only my face was visible!

I was given the anaesthetic.

★ ★ ★

'Where am I? Have I been done? Can I drink?' I was back in the ward. One minute I was awake and then I was asleep again.

'Is she still, 'nil by mouth'?'

The food lady was going away with the food.

'I'm starving! I need food!'

'You'll probably be sick.' The nurse smiled at me, then put her hand on the trolley and looked at the woman. 'All right. Try some. What have you got? Give her something light.'

I swallowed jelly followed by chicken soup and kept both down.

The day had gone when I woke up and saw John, my teacher friend from my previous school, at the foot of my bed. He'd come all the way from Putney to visit me. No one else came.

After Dr Amery had been to see me the next morning a young Philippino nurse appeared at my bedside and gave me her card. She said she was a Macmillan nurse and that she would be there to help me if I needed her. No one else came until I was allowed out three days later and my friend Pat came to drive me home and stay that first night with me.

Dear Jesus, I'm glad I've got Pat. She's managed to leave her husband and mother in order to look after me. She's bought and cooked the food and has done all she can to take away my fears. What would I do without her love and care?

Where were the Sisters or my family? I no longer belonged to the nuns. My family? They had their own problems. Besides, they had got used to me being looked after in the convent since I was fourteen.

After ten days I had to return to see my surgeon. No one spoke in the waiting room. Judy, my Macmillan nurse, was there. But she was there for other people too. The thing was everybody else had someone with them. But maybe they were very sick.

I have only had a lump out and it probably wasn't cancer at all.

My name was called out. Was it? Judy stood up and so did I. Mr Amery came out of his room and Judy let me go through the door first.

'How do you feel? You'll be a bit sore for a time. To be expected. Now we have the results of the tests back. We found abnormal cells. All contained in the one lump.'

There must have been a mistake. Is he saying I've got cancer? I can't have cancer! Why's everyone looking at me? Am I supposed to say something?

'I . . . abnormal?' I struggled.

'Malignant tumour. Cancer. But it's probably been caught in time and hasn't spread.'

Jesus, why should I believe that? You said I most likely didn't have cancer! You said you could have put a needle in and the lump would disappear! Liar!

'Now, just to make sure that all the badness has been removed we need to take out some of your lymph nodes and make sure they are clear. Unfortunately we can only do this by operating again as soon as possible. That's the best thing to do.' He looked at me, then he looked at Judy and Judy looked back at me. 'Judy's the expert at explaining all about that. You can ask all the questions you want when you think of them. All right?'

I was outside his door and sitting with Judy. She said she was going home to the Philippines but Jane would be there for me. We'd go now and meet her.

Jane phoned my doctor. I went home. A district nurse came to my house. I cried and said lots of things. She listened, sympathised, reassured me and went away. I phoned my sister. My mother phoned me. My brother phoned. They were all sad. But I was alone with my cancer.

'You look so well!'

Jesus, if anyone says that to me again I'll scream, hit them and shout! You can't see cancer, you bloody fools! Ejeets! That's the whole point. It gets in without you knowing!

The scar on my left breast was just healing when I had my lymph nodes ripped out. They became infected. My arm swelled up. I had to call an emergency doctor out on a Sunday. Another day I went up to Casualty and had it drained. I had a ten-week course of radiotherapy in St Luke's Cancer Hospital. Volunteers from the hospital offered transport or else I was picked up by ambulance.

Alone, anxious and fearful, I struggled to cope. The summer of 1995 was extremely hot and often when I returned from radiotherapy I just managed to unlock my door, get to the kitchen and push some food into my mouth before I collapsed on the floor of my front room and fell asleep.

I was continually asking for information, books or leaflets about cancer. I phoned all the help lines, sent away for the booklets and plagued Jane, the Macmillan nurse, with my endless questions. I asked to go for psychotherapy because I wondered what it was that I had done wrong and I believed that this disease had affected my whole person. In both St Luke's and Frimley Park Hospital I was given appointments to see counsellors. Counsellor Gail Maguire and Radiotherapist Charlotte McDowell who now manage The Fountain Centre in The Royal Surrey Hospital were particularly helpful.

Lord God, why am I so angry? My body is disfigured. The breasts that I had not touched or even looked at and had hoped had been saved intact for a normal life are no longer appealing. The left one has been cut into and is sagging and under my arm is numb and gashed. Am I being punished for leaving the convent? The hopes I had nurtured of meeting and maybe one day marrying the man of my dreams are being crushed.

I hate medicine, potions and pills and yet I had to agree to go on the drug Tamoxifen whose manufacturers listed half a page of possible side effects. If I wanted to live and increase my chances of preventing cancer from reoccurring I had no choice in this matter. So I became bloated, tired and sluggish as well as crippled by fear. My eyesight was going. I had no reason for getting up any morning. I wrote my Will and applied for and accepted early retirement from teaching on the grounds of ill-health. Now that I had accepted that I was about to die I no longer cared about anything.

It was then I started writing poetry.

CANCER

Cancer!
Horror of horrors!
Fewer tomorrows.
How did it happen?
Questions and answers, anger and
    blame.
Insidiously creeping without physical
    pain.
Cell reproduction misses a stage
Forms its own pattern,
Peculiar, diseased.
Lumps, cysts and blockage.
Silently creeping without physical pain.
Cancer detected,
Sorrow of sorrows!
How to accept it, how to explain?
Have I a future? Why this? *Why me?*
Lumps, lumpectomy and lymph nodes
    removing.
Anti-oestrogen, Tamoxifen.
Radiotherapy, psychotherapy,
Systematically curing with mental strain.
Now I've produced it will I do so again?

32

Death

Lonesome and lonely in the dark and weighed down by my heavy-tog duvet, I was depressed. It was the same type of depression that I had experienced that night at the end of August 1997 when Princess Diana died. Yet another summer alone, pretending that almost seven years of searching for someone special to love me did not matter, had taken its toll.

I replayed the Diana night while I tossed and turned and reached for my earphones. Wired up, I was startled! Diana was in a crash! I switched from station to station seeing the same scene: a crushed Mercedes limousine. She was still alive? They said so. Suddenly stricken with sadness I sat up and storm-sized tears spilled, wetting my night-dress. One soggy tissue followed another on to the carpet. Wanting to tear my earpieces away I listened to the constant repetition of the same surmise. No one seemed to know if she would survive and then . . . they said she wouldn't! And she didn't!

Back beneath the covers, crying through that night, I knew I was despairing at the shattering of my own fairytale dreams of becoming a princess and being taken up the aisle on the arm of a passionate prince.

I had watched the cortege and visited the scene of the floral tributes in sombre mood. It was a bleak August indeed. My friend Anne Marie F had asked me to accompany her to Kensington Gardens to join the procession of people of all ages. Were they crying for themselves and broken promises or unfulfilled dreams?

I remember coming away from the banks of fading flowers and catching sight of a woman in black resembling Queen Victoria walk in front of me into the shadows. This vision startled me so suddenly and disappeared so fast that I felt weak and unable to tell my friend. Then I felt silly and so afraid that no one would believe me that I kept it to myself.

Dear Lord, why am I torturing myself replaying and reliving all this now? Why can't I recall all the progress I have made and the success I have achieved in what I called my catching-up years? Six years ago I had to queue outside a phone box to contact anyone and now I have my own answering machine. That's it, Jesus! That's what triggered all this off!

I threw my covers off and pulled my sweaty nightdress away from me.

Dear God, was it the message on my phone that had plunged me back into gloom?

★ ★ ★

'*Sister Marion, sorry to be the bearer of sad news but Sister Madeleine Hammond has passed away and the reception of her body is to take place in Streatham on Friday evening at seven and the funeral Mass on the following day at eleven thirty. Sister Helen D'Arcy is also struggling to stay alive. Would you mind informing Margaret, Maura and Anna? In case you don't recognise my brogue, this is Norma.*'

Why should I allow myself to be sad and miserable again? I had gone through so much trauma these past years as well as three operations and a course of radiotherapy. So why should I respond to the phone message? But I did.

I drove the three other ex-nuns from our Order, who lived near me, in my blue Rover 111i, to Streatham convent for the Prayers for the Repose of the Soul of Sister Madeleine. I was not tuned in to their reminiscing as we travelled because I was thinking about Maeve, hoping that she would be there. She had not kept contact with me since I moved to live in Camberley and teach in Farnborough, but somehow I had heard that she had formed a Catechetical group with progressive ideas. Rumours had also reached me that she was busy on other ventures, but nobody appeared to have real evidence of what was really going on.

Probably the only thing my three travelling companions had in common was that we had been members of the same Religious Congregation. However, on one of the rare occasions that we went out for a meal together we agreed to refer to ourselves as 'Firm Friends' only so that we could substitute the word 'firm' for 'convent'. We hoped that by so doing we would succeed in protecting our privacy when reminiscing in public places. It was bad enough being Irish without being labelled as ex-nuns as well. This certainly stopped 'Look-Out Maura' from constantly interrupting conversations at table with instructions like, 'Shish! Will ye shish! Don't give the game away! That couple over there are listening in to your every word!'

Confident in an olive green, well-tailored suit and matching brown accessories, I rang the convent doorbell. All four of us were well groomed. It was important to let the Sisters see that our second choice in life was successful.

Grown tall in her high heels, slender Margaret turned impishly on the semicircle we formed on the doorstep asking, 'Guess who'll open the door?'

Suddenly regressed, we chorused, 'Mary Brown!'

And she did, opening her arms wide to embrace us, saying 'Ye're great to come!'

Once inside it was as if I had never left. The incense, the 'Long Live Jesus' greeting, the shades and shadows and subdued tones. I wanted to open doors, peep and wander, but it was no longer my house. Sister Monica was shunting us into chapel amid smiles and nods. My blouse was clinging to my back but I didn't want to ruin my image by removing my jacket. Tugging at my short skirt after genuflecting, I handed out the leaflets for the Service to my three confused-looking companions. I was surmising from their bewildered expressions that they shared my feelings.

There was no sign of Maeve.

We sang the words of well-known hymns so loudly in our bench that the people in front of us turned, presumably to see if we were wearing habits. How else would we be so familiar with this selection of in-house melodies?

'True to the spirit of both Saint John Bosco and Saint Mary Mazarello, Sister Madeleine shone as a splendid example of compassion for the poor and needy. May she now enjoy the reward of having generously dedicated sixty years of her life as a professed Sister united with and for Christ Jesus, Our Lord.'

This was the tone of one prayer after another, recited by a Sister, the Sister Superior, a past pupil and a Cooperator lined up solemnly behind the heavy brown rostrum. Then holy Sister Monica invited anyone in the congregation to add their own petition to these bidding-prayers.

Why are these pious platitudes being attributed to someone I know to have been rebellious and anti-authority all her years, Jesus? I can't constrain the venomous bile erupting through my trembling body!

Then I heard myself exclaiming: 'I am glad to be here tonight to rejoice that the fun-loving Sister Madeleine who washed the pots and pans with us in the back pantry and who was not afraid to face up to the challenges life presented her with, is finally being rewarded in heaven. I look forward to Mass tomorrow when we will no doubt be singing the rousing hymn, 'Glory, Glory Alleluia!' that she repeatedly requested to be rendered with great gusto at her funeral.'

Nudges, pats on my shoulders, waves and smiles assured me that those who really knew Sister Madeleine were delighted that the pretence was over and the genuine ensuing prayers made me feel that I had been a catalyst for life in an otherwise morbid atmosphere. However, the piercing look that sedate Sister Marie, clad in her full-length black habit, turned in my direction told me that I certainly could not count on her approval. But cutting glances from other newly professed Sisters only served to make my spine tingle — I was a little excited that I had influence but still fearful and wary that I was being observed by these young fervent sisters and could be responsible for influencing them before they had enough experience to form their own opinions.

Once out in the corridor I decided to break down other barriers by bursting into the kitchen and chatting to an overworked and exhausted-looking Sister Brigid busily straining the chips and turning battered cod. There was a twinkle in her tired eyes and a smile on her skinny face. Her claw-like arms swiped grease from her crinkly brow as she cackled amusingly, 'You never lost it, Marion! Wouldn't you come back and cheer us up? Sure you're like a tonic, d'you know that?'

Sister Marie, pulling open the door at that

344

moment interrupted with, 'Marion, we have reserved a place for you in the refectory with the other former sisters.'

Fuming, but conscious that Brigid had to live under this regime, I managed to give her a knowing wink while following Sister Marie to join the others.

On entering the dining room I looked around at tables of laity and Sisters intermingling and unceremoniously dismissed Sister Marie by pointing and saying for all to hear, 'Well, if it isn't Sister Mary Brown and friends beckoning me!'

It was then the fun began.

'Well, how are things? Is it as good as it's cracked up to be, Marion?'

'What exactly do you mean by *it*?' I teased.

'Do you have a place of your own?'

'I was sorry to hear you had breast cancer. But you're looking well. Are you over it now?'

'Aren't you lonely though? You that thrives on an audience, alone? But perhaps you're not and you've discovered true love? Have you?'

A buxom, red-faced woman from the next table tapped my back and proclaimed to all, 'Are you the Sister Marion that taught my Seán? Have you left the nuns now?'

'Mrs Gillian, isn't it?'

With visions of her demon offspring in

345

mind, I replied loud and clearly, 'Yes, I have moved on, married, and inherited two intelligent boys from a rich husband and reside in leafy Surrey. I believe it is referred to as the Brokers' Belt. And how are you?'

Wobbling her false teeth back into place, she mumbled, 'Good' as she turned round to her table, and giggles and sniggers hissed from my companions who correctly suspected that my brag had been concocted to put an end to her potential to spread malicious rumours.

I forgot about my three fellow travellers until windows were being opened to extract the clinging smell of batter and chips and the folks at our table, having avoided hints about helping with the washing up, were now trying to ignore signals to send me home.

Eventually, going through the front door, I delighted in looking over my shoulder at the shrouded Sister Marie to jibe, 'You'll be delighted to know that, because I am retired now, I'll be able to help give Sister Madeleine a good send-off tomorrow!'

Thrilled that I had succeeded in making my presence felt, I became aware from what the others said on the journey back that Sister Helen D'Arcy was not expected to survive the night.

★ ★ ★

Maeve's defiant stance made me slow down as I swung into the drive the next day. Firmly grounded, with the crown of her head towering above what looked like a group of executive women being addressed by her. Their poise and smart trouser-suit attire could have fooled others into supposing that they were being briefed by a spin-doctor for an important press release. But on closer inspection I recognised them all to be our Sisters.

Turning to see me, Maeve smiled and swaggered over in fashionable suede boots and suit. She had the lot: a leopard-patterned chiffon scarf and a handbag! All that was missing were the earrings and make-up and I was not sure that I didn't detect traces of that.

Snuggling me into her warm embrace and Opium perfume, Maeve outlined the tactics we were to adopt that day.

'Sister Helen D'Arcy died early this morning and they want to save money by making it a double funeral!'

'They wouldn't? What about her relatives?'

'No. They won't! We've got to stop it going ahead. That's what we were planning, and we'll succeed. Come, we're going in now to confront the powers that be.'

As we unceremoniously went through the

French doors, I caught sight of an elderly woman in a straight grey coat and brown furry hat at the lectern and others seated in a semicircle, with two coffins facing the altar. All the women were dressed in an array of colours and fashions available in Oxfam shops. It was the Sisters in grey, black and white habits intermingled with them that made me realise that these were all Sisters from communities of our Order and the one at the lectern was Sister Eileen, the same Sister Superior who had reprimanded me for not wearing my veil only a few years before!

I sat down and then realised Maeve and the others had disappeared. A few minutes later voices were raised in the corridor — I presumed it was Maeve & Co arguing their case — but the two coffins remained and the robed clergy began to proceed to the altar behind the cross singing, 'Lord Of All Hopefulness.'

There was no sign of Maeve and group. Where had they gone? The obviously hastily duplicated Order of Mass leaflets with the names of both Sister Madeleine and Sister Helen D'Arcy were being sung but the hymns — 'The Lord is my Shepherd' and 'Lord For Tomorrow' — were all so general. All right for anyone's funeral but not appertaining to anyone in particular. This was all so impersonal. Stunned, I stayed to hear the bland bidding prayers, which did not reflect the characters of those being prayed for. But I shuddered with rage when I saw Sister Elaine Webb mount the step to give the eulogy and was fit to do somersaults up the aisle in the nude when she enthused about her own achievements in life! She had always been capable of singing her own praises but today it sounded as if she had used a 'Hints For Self-Assertion' pamphlet as her text!

Furious, I left before Mass was over to discover Maeve and friends driving off in their red Cortina. I followed them to a restaurant further down the road and, having seen me in her car mirror, Maeve signalled for me to join them.

Changed days, I thought as I emerged from my car, conscious that although the floral dress and wine jacket I was wearing were bought from a high-street store as opposed to a charity shop, they were neither stylish or figure-flattering.

These well-dressed, confident women paraded inside and put in their orders without hesitation, certainty beaming from their relaxed, reassured faces.

The agenda for the discussion could have been 'The Price Is Right' since each of the five took turns to outline the state of play they had so far reached in negotiating the amount of money they would get if they left the Order.

'I know for a fact that a friend of mine who is about to leave the Irish Sisters of Clemency is to be given forty thousand in cash and a house in a secluded complex in Mayo.'

'Wow! Is that sterling or euros?' inquired Sister Dympna, finishing off her melon and kiwi starter.

'And all our lot is attempting to fob us off with is a measly twenty thousand if there is no support available from the individual's family,' commented Connie, wincing at the bitterness of grapefruit and then reaching for the brown sugar.

'I mean, after cutting yourself off — in my case for twenty years — from your family, is it right to be encouraged to turn to a married brother struggling to bring up four of his own, to ask for financial assistance?' Anya's pupils were popping in and out, her eyelids flipping open and closed.

Once the main meal was eaten, coffee served and amounts in various settlements aired, Maeve took control. Seated in the centre of an alcove partitioned off from the rest of the restaurant, she informed all of the progress she had made by contacting people like a lawyer allocated to advise religious on their positions, and a certain Sister Zita in the Advent Group who offered counselling at a comparatively cheap rate.

'Be sure your Income Tax has been paid and you send away for a Pension Forecast before you sign off,' I warned as I came to realise why Maeve had involved me in this meeting.

This raised unforeseen matters to be addressed and I was able to reveal what it had been like for priests and nuns I had commiserated with since I had left. There were howls of laughter when I recounted how Father Paddy, being interviewed for a catering position in Homebase, was asked how many people he had experience of cooking for — and came up with the figure of over a hundred because he had visions of himself putting on that number of boiled eggs for the community retreat breakfast!

'Well, what else could the guy do? I mean, saying he was good at preaching wouldn't have exactly enhanced his CV, would it?' Maeve said, sounding what was a serious note for all of us as she gathered up her file and stood ready to close this session.

Out on the doorstep again, throwing the car keys to Sister Sonia, Maeve put her arm through mine explaining, 'Marion and I have to catch up. Ye'll find yeer own way back?'

But my hopes of having intimate exchanges were soon set aside when Maeve pleaded, 'Marion, please, would you drive me to Antic Answers in Sunningdale? I have an appointment there at four. I was delighted you followed us because I don't want anyone finding out my business.'

Antic Answers was an antique shop so at first I surmised it might have something to do with her late aunt's possessions, but even then I wondered why there needed to be secretiveness and, besides, by her vow of poverty Maeve should have no financial gain accrued to her.

She did not say much on the short journey and when the security bell alerted the bearded man that we had arrived in the up-market shop, I realised that this was the sort of place where valuable deals were done. Pretending to potter about, hardly daring to touch mahogany, oak, intricate designs and highly polished surfaces, after some time I spied Maeve being handed a cheque and had my suspicions confirmed.

Back in the car I challenged her and she bound me to silence by declaring that since I had left she had become aware that she would never get a just amount of money when she left the Order.

'The price is not going to be right until

someone lets outsiders know how little most nuns get when they leave the convent and who is going to be fool enough to do that? Besides, even if they did who would care? No, it is each one for herself.'

'So, what's your solution? What were you selling there?'

Sitting sideways in the front of my car and holding my praying hands in hers, she gazed in my eyes and said firmly, 'I have started up my own antiques business. I have a hideout in which I store my finds safely. I opened a bank account to manage my affairs. I am sorry I didn't tell you this before but I didn't know if you would approve and I couldn't risk that.'

33

Sicilian Scandal

'Anne, I'm desperate to talk to you. I'm sorry. I've been waiting in the car.'

Looking thoroughly exhausted and hauling her bulging bag, Anne tried to keep up with me and eventually flopped into the front seat of the Micra Alley. It was Monday and she had taken PE followed by playground duty. On top of that she had spent the previous week away in Hastings with forty six to seven-year-olds.

'I know you'll be recovering from the kids' hols. But there's something that I need to tell you urgently . . . that's if you're not too tired. I did leave a message on your answering machine — '

'What is it, Marion? I'm sorry. I'm — '

'Yes, I know. In fact, maybe you're too exhausted . . . '

'No, I'm OK. The children were their usual lively selves. They were fine. But tell me. You look ashen.'

We drove a short distance up a hill to a more secluded part of the Streatham

Common, got out and sat close to each other on a bench.

'Remember when our friend Nora recommended that I go away to a lovely house run by some priests in Sicily? Remember, she and her husband had been on holiday there and considered that, because it was so safe and wholesome, it would be an ideal place for me to recuperate?

'It all sounded very good. She has always been a very caring person. But something awful must have happened. Your eyes are popping out of our head. You poor dear!'

With that Anne's arms sprang round me.

'Anne, one of the priests took advantage of me.'

'God, no! I don't believe it!'

'Yes, I'm very embarrassed and angry over what happened.'

'That bad?'

I cast my eyes down and in a subdued tone went on to tell how Father Fabio had taken advantage of me. Falteringly I managed to relate what had happened.

After punctuating this account with appropriate exclamations, I banged the bench and said, 'I'm not letting him get away with this! Maybe because his English was not very good he may not have understood every word I said, but you don't need to master a language

355

to know that you don't touch a person up and attempt to . . . '

'Yes! The cheek of him!'

'These bloody priests!' I was shouting, forgetting that anyone passing could hear me. 'What I found very strange though was that when I returned I phoned Sister Josephine in Rome and told her what had happened and do you know what she said?'

'Well, she is very kind after all — she used to be our Superior here. She'll have been helpful.'

'That's what I expected. But she told me to pray!'

'Fat lot of good — excuse me — that's a cop out! Was she afraid of upsetting the priests?'

'Yes, exactly. So then I demanded to meet with the Provincial of the English branch of the Order of those priests and I gave them a written account of everything.'

'That must have been embarrassing enough.'

'Yes, it was. I felt quite traumatised. In fact, the whole thing was awful.'

'But who was there?'

'There were two priests that I didn't know and a woman who they told me was a member of the Child Protection Team. It was left to me to provide the agenda. I gave each of those there an A4 sheet on which I had outlined eleven points that I expected to be fulfilled as a result of that meeting.'

'Child Protection Team to address your adult complaint? What was their attitude? Were they sympathetic?'

'No, not one of them seemed to show any sincere feelings for me. In fact, the priest who said he was to report back to the Father General of the Order in Rome had a sneering smirk on his face.'

'That is appalling. Surely the *woman* felt for you?'

'Yes, of the three of them she did say a few kind words but then afterwards proved that she had no authority to actually do anything. At my own cost I could phone her if I wished to speak to her but she lives way down in Devon.'

'Marion, you know that you need to get some professional help, some counselling. That, as well as forcing those priests to be accountable!'

The traffic was building up now around the edge of the common. I stood up.

But before getting up to get back in the nearby car, Anne stamped her foot into the cement slab under our bench saying, 'You'll have to get him! This is sexual harassment and you *must* get this priest moved! What you said about that other young Englishwoman there receiving the same abuse must spur you on. But you must know Religious Orders are so scared of anything to do with sexual abuse that they go into denial.'

The rush hour was in full swing when I dropped Anne at the tube before I headed off.

As I edged bumper to bumper, I prayed: *Lord God, why is the Catholic Church so adamant about the vow of chastity for its religious and clergy? You know your priests are weak and so many break their vows.*

Little did I know then that years were to go by during which I tried to get the Church hierarchy to answer for what had happened to me in Sicily, contacting in turn the Provincial of Salesian Priests in England; Archbishop Vincent Nichols, Archdiocese of Birmingham; Cardinal Cormac Murphy O'Connor, Westminster Diocese; and the Rector Major of the Salesians in the *Generalate* in Rome.

All to no avail.

34

Exposure

'Marion, Marion, is that you?'

'Des, since I live alone who else could it be?' I had just clattered down the stairs as quickly as I could from the bathroom.

'It's just that I left you a message on your answering machine and . . . well, are you watching *Richard and Judy*?'

'You're talking about the Short Story Competition, aren't you? Yes, I just popped up to the bathroom during the adverts.'

'So how about it? Why don't you send the short story you told me you wrote for your Writing Group about the Sicily incident?'

'You mean, 'publish and be damned'? It's a good idea but what puts me off is that if — and it's a big if — I ever got published, I *would* be damned!'

'No, you wouldn't! You need to get it out of your system and this might be a good way of tackling it. Shaming these priests?'

'Now, Des, you know that I've been using writing as a kind of therapy, but going public could lose me friends.'

'Not real friends. Besides, you could change all the names and places and just enter it as a competition piece. Use a pseudonym. That way you'd help yourself health-wise and you might even win! I mean, you'd most likely win!'

'All that plámásing will get you anywhere! I'll tell you what I'll do. I'll change the names etc on the version of it I have and send it on to you to see what you think. OK?'

'Promise me you'll do that today? No pressure but it will have to be sent off to *Richard and Judy* by the weekend!'

★ ★ ★

Part of me really needed to get my account published. I was conscious that I still carried a good deal of anger since I had suffered the sexual abuse and been ignored about the matter, and having had cancer I wanted to protect myself from a reoccurrence, but I was also afraid of everyone knowing my business and judging me. However, I decided to do what my brother suggested and later that day I sent him the story I had written.

Beast and the Beauty

Thrusting splurting red flames into the night

sky, Etna wore her collar of snow as we circled her on our way from Catania Airport.

With more of a smirk than a smile, olive-skinned Don Fabio seemed as hot-blooded and passionate as the elements. Fired up and ready to erupt, was he frustrated with my cool responses?

'Sicilians show their feelings. The climate is hot — they are hot! You are in Sicily now.'

One hand steered the old car around the volcano while the other groped my knee. He wasn't wearing his collar.

Sure, he had waited at the airport even though my plane was delayed well past midnight, but he hadn't offered to carry my case and he looked so short and smarmy.

Nora had warned me to arrive in Mafia-land during the day and it was not from lack of pleading that I failed to change my flight.

Maybe if I declared all my cards he would stop. But telling him that I'd left the convent after being a nun for thirty-three years seemed to egg him on. Worse! When I said that I'd come on holiday to recover from cancer he asked for details and when I struggled for the Italian for 'breast' he stretched out a probing hand.

Dear Jesus, what'll I do? Nora assured me that I'd be safe with these priests. After all, hadn't Don Bosco set up the outfit to help youth live chaste lives?

'Once they realise that you have been a member of their Order all these years, you'll be well away,' she'd said.

Don Fabio quizzed on: 'Do you think nuns and priests should show their feelings? Here in Sicily we always have but now I understand there is a growing realisation in the Church that we Religious are no different from lay people. We have to be like the people and show that we love and hate just like others do. It's only natural. That's how God made us, isn't it? You agree?'

We were orbiting the perimeter of the enormous volcano in the middle of the night. Going round and round in his tinny car, we were sizzling and smelling much like black puddings in a frying pan. The swarthy sky stretched into infinity and I was becoming more and more scared of being tossed into the flames of this frenzied priest-man.

Then there was street lighting and we came to an abrupt halt at the side of a massively high church structure. He jumped out and opened the boot.

'Take your belongings and follow me.'

I heaved my case along while he rattled a bundle of keys and raced over marble floors and up a wide staircase, putting low lights on

362

and off en route to the bedrooms. I was desperate to lock this apparently insatiable beast out of mine.

He pointed. 'Yours is between mine and Martello's. But don't worry about him, he's a sick man. Diabetic.'

He hugged me through the narrow bedroom door, into the room and onto the balcony, pointing out how close we were to the thrusting pinnacle. He squeezed my waist and smeared me with kisses. How was it he didn't feel my goose pimples as he tugged me closer and manoeuvred me back through the door towards the bed?

'Where was the cancer? Let me compare the two!' He pulled up my top and cupped, fondled and fingered. Frozen in horror, I could hardly react.

'No! Please!' I pulled away and made sure my shoulder bag was strategically placed. He wrenched at the bag.

'No! No! Don't!'

He ignored my plea, cradled my face in his hands and smothered my cries with kisses. Clearly chastity, celibacy or running a sanctuary for young people was not going to inhibit this volatile beast.

Lord God, if I hit him what will he do? How can I stop him?

'You must want a shower. Here, let me

show you how it works. I'll help you. Have you got soap? Ah, but first let me show you my bed.'

He coaxed me forward into his room. The duvet was folded down. He leered while he slithered his fingers between mine. He dragged a towel from the top of a cupboard and holding it up said, 'I can dry you down too!' Then leading me back to my room, he closed the door and flung me onto the bed. He tried to unzip my trousers but I managed to push him away.

'*No! No!*' I screamed.

He let go. 'Why so angry? Don't be afraid. You're tired. You sleep. Don't worry, I'll look after you.' More kisses plonked. 'I'll bring your breakfast in bed. Just lie there and I'll take care of you.'

After he left my room I felt like mown grass, bagged and ready for the dump. I bolted the door and window shutters. I searched for peeping-holes or cracks. Eventually I managed to undress enough to wash and then snatched some sleep, propped up against the pillow. My alarm woke me at seven to heat already sneaking under the shutters. Gasping for air and anxious to establish my exact location, I tried to fold back half a shutter very quietly. While I took a deep breath the lapping of waves drew my attention down over the rock cliff to Bella Isola, set like a jewel in the turquoise sea inlet.

But then a cold shiver sliced through me as I glimpsed a slight movement. It was him! Only a low iron balcony-divider prevented him from jumping over on to my side. Half clothed in vest and trousers, he grinned and prowled nearer.

'Oh, you're already dressed! You could have stayed in bed. Why don't you go back and I'll bring you coffee?' he almost sang.

'No, I want to go out. I don't eat much in the morning,' I lied.

'Bed and breakfast! You've had the bed, now the breakfast and anything else you want. Let me take care of you!'

I drew back, closed the shutters tight and cradled myself on the wicker chair. How was I to get out of this man's clutches? Accommodation in touristy Taormina is very costly even before the holiday season begins. He'd agreed on a bargain deal and now I knew why. I scratched my hands through my hair, realising that I was trapped.

What if I kept out of his way? I'd find a supermarket and eat in my room.

I crept downstairs, in the direction of the door I'd come through the previous evening.

'This way, this way! Come, come!'

Froglike, he sprang forward, kissing and rubbing. He took me by the hand and led me unwillingly into the refectory to Don Martello. They both ogled and shook their heads. Obviously this was not the first time he had behaved in this manner. Were they in this together?

Don Fabio directed me towards the coffee. The jug felt lukewarm. This was probably how they drank it. I sat and reached for the bread. It was hard. Were those artichokes they were eating? Vegetables for breakfast! That's what he reminded me of. He smelt like an artichoke. He felt like one. Slithery, layered, fleshy and slimy green.

'Thanks but I'm not hungry and I want to go out. I'll find my own way.'

'I can take you out. We can drive somewhere?'

'No, thank you. I want to wander.'

They both stood and Fabio caught my hand and led me. Once in the corridor his arm was around my waist and he snuggled and kissed. At the door, there was another smacker and then the holding of hands while he gazed into my eyes.

'Is there a key I can use to get in and out?'

He pressed a spare key in my hand.

I felt sickened and longed to run away but where? The path led down to Piazza Aprile.

This overlooked a cliff with a sheer drop down to one of the most spectacular views in Sicily. When I turned round and looked to my left I could see fuming Mount Etna. Flicking flames in juxtaposition to snow!

In spite of being weak, I almost ran through the arches past the shopping area and made my way down the cliff. Tears clouded out the beauty of this incredible place and forced me to stop and sit on a rough rocky shelf away from the path. As most people rode in the cable car, I pondered my plight out of sight.

As the tears splattered, I relived the day I discovered that I had the lump.

I had replayed this trauma every Maundy Thursday to Easter Tuesday for the last five years: the nurse who carried out the examination telling me that I had three lumps, me comparing myself to Christ on the cross awaiting death, walking home alone, having to endure a long wait through the holiday weekend not knowing if the lump was cancerous and feeling too weak to walk or eat. My mother advising me not to worry. She'd had lumps and look at her, wasn't she nearing seventy and a smoker to boot?

There were the tests, followed by surgery to remove the lump, surrounding breast tissue and lymph nodes. But worst of all was the realization that I had cancer. Then there was the course of radiotherapy. A year later I had to have two more incisions to rid me of polyps in my uterus and then there was the epidural for the back pain. The latter were probably necessitated because of the side effects I experienced from the drug Tamoxifen.

Most of this I faced alone. Having pushed my family away during the convent years, how could I expect anything else?

'Get away from it all. Give yourself a break. In fact, reward yourself for being so brave. Why don't you go to Sicily? Yes, there's a really safe place run by priests. Although Taormina is a popular tourist place, it's the ideal spot and you'd be able to holiday there at a cheaper rate.'

That's what my friend Nora had advised when I told her that depression was once more beginning to set in as yet another Easter approached.

Sandalled feet springing from rock to rock brought a dark-skinned deer-like young man down the cliff. I leapt and followed at a safe distance. We were isolated. He turned and waited and answered my 'Buon giorno' with 'Merci'. Maybe he was Algerian. What was he doing in Taormina? All he had to do was hit me and let me roll to my death. He held out his hand and led me to the path and down to more level ground. Then he waved goodbye and quickened his pace.

Half an hour later I tried ordering coffee. That's when I learnt that my trip down the cliff had taken me into Nexus where they sprinkle their Italian with Greek. I walked and walked, aware that there were many lone men on the loose.

Although the turquoise sea and poppy-filled orange groves were inviting, I needed to get back up to Taormina to shop for food to eat in my room. The hearty breakfasts I had planned to stave off my hunger were not to be and because I felt threatened and vulnerable I planned to stock up and lock up. But after surviving thirty-three years of convent life, followed by my cancer time, I could surely manage for five days. Yes, I'd keep with groups of people when I was out and eat alone behind closed doors.

'*Dove il supermercato, per favore?*' was responded to with raised hands and shaking of the heads but eventually I found enough biscuits, cheese and fruit in a grocer's shop.

For two days I sneaked upstairs and locked my room unmolested, but on the third day Don Fabio pounced on me as I crept down the stairs. The kiss was slapped on and he held my hand over his trousers as he suddenly discovered that he had to zip up. Again he led me into their refectory and seated me next to him and opposite Don Martello. He handed me a plate and invited me to help myself. I scanned the platters of cheese, beans, various pulses and a good deal of fruit. The two of them smirked while eyeing the sparsely clad females on the TV adverts. I ate little, responded to their questions and made my exit as quickly and as politely as possible.

The following night I realised that the manner in which Don Fabio had treated me was probably habitual. I had returned earlier than on previous days and opened a door into a room that I had to traverse on my way to my bedroom to find a beautiful, young, blonde, girl being embraced by Don Fabio — an English girl who had appeared earlier that day with an older English couple who had succeeded in getting her accommodation with the priests while they were staying with friends. He scowled at me. I used her 'Hello' as an excuse to help translate. She smiled as he lost interest and excused himself.

Don Fabio officiated at the Easter Services and I received Holy Communion from his hands. Later, from the distance of my balcony, I drank carafes of disillusionment as I witnessed an elaborate enactment of the

Way of the Cross led by him across the Piazza Aprile.

Each day that I survived convinced me that I could endure another. Aware that I was avoiding him Don Fabio ignored me. Although that suited me well.

On the last day I dreaded having to find him in order to settle my bill. He ordered me to his office and demanded much more than we had agreed. Then he informed me that since he would not be available to take me to the airport I would have to pay a driver. I paid him what he exacted.

I said goodbye politely but as I turned to go he forced a final hug and kiss on me.

When we finally reached Catania I almost threw my last lire at the erratic driver so I had to beg for water during my two-hour stopover in Rome.

But I was glad that I had kicked the Taormina dust from my feet.

★ ★ ★

That was the story my brother wanted me to submit to *Richard & Judy*. But I didn't. Instead I began to consider writing a book.

35

I Wish

Scene: The Late Late Show, RTE Studios, Dublin

Host Pat Kenny: Would you please welcome blonde and bubbly ex-nun Marion who left the convent sixteen years ago and has now had her book *Dropping the Habit* about 'her time inside' published.

Marion: I was in for life, sir! I left home a month before my fifteenth birthday and was detained for thirty-two years. That's almost as long as Jesus Christ was alive!

Pat Kenny: So tell us about your book.

Marion: My book has gone through various stages. It was written primarily for therapeutic reasons. It's grown from a set of vignettes and memories to a biography and now to an autobiography.

Pat Kenny: Therapeutic reasons? So why go public?

372

Marion: I thrive on attention! *I do*, you know. Ask any of the nuns. Anyone will tell you I spent a good deal of my time acting about, singing, writing poems and generally looking for attention! The parents of the children I taught were forever telling me that I was not like many of the other Sisters.

Pat Kenny: Now dare I ask you — were you — *are* you as a nun and as a woman treated well by the Church?

Marion: No! I have met and indeed have befriended many decent priests and bishops. But my overall opinion is that the Catholic hierarchy with its bishops, priests, the Pope — especially this new one Pope Benedict — rarely appreciates the role of women.

Pat Kenny: What about the nuns themselves?

Marion: I'm glad you asked that. Some of the nuns I lived with were — *are* narrow-minded thwarted spinsters, many are probably lesbian and others were — *are* inspirational. And myself? Well, I'm a product of a certain strict Catholic upbringing, doctrines and teachings. Hailing from Limerick, as I do, means that I carry a lot of baggage too — as you'll know if you've read Frank McCourt's portrayal or should I say 'betrayal' of Limerick in *Angela's Ashes!* But you may not know that Limerick is referred to, up and down the country, as 'Stab City'! Oh, so you do! But then none of us chooses where we're born.

Pat Kenny: When you were only fourteen plus and just entered the convent, were you lonesome? Did you ever feel like going back home? Could you have done?

Marion: Oh well! I remember one Visiting Sunday. We were allowed visitors from two to four on the first Sunday of each month. Well, this Sunday when I walked my parents and my Uncle Brendan back down to the big gates which led out of the grounds, my uncle caught my hand saying, 'Let's make a run for it! Home we go!' Uncle Brendan was a great, liberal-minded, fun-loving man who had tried to talk me out of entering. So he was only half-joking when he said let's make a run for it. But, you know, I didn't want to leave the nuns then.

Pat Kenny: Do you feel any guilt for leaving

eventually? For breaking your vows?

Marion: Yes, I divorced Jesus! But gee! He's got thousands of spouses!

Pat Kenny: And there're no children involved! But am I right in saying you looked angry when I said that?

Marion: Almost every woman wants children and I missed out.

Pat Kenny: You could have got married when you left?

Marion: I'm still looking! Maybe I'll be approached after this exposé!

Pat Kenny: Marion, who do you blame most for what life has thrown at you?

Marion: No-one. Life is made up of a series of decisions.

Pat Kenny: So you reckon you were old enough to decide at fourteen going on fifteen?

Marion: No, but I could have left before I was fully committed. I entered as an aspirant, then became a postulant, then a novice. The whole process took six years. Only then did I take my vows. And even then, you renew those vows several times over a period of six or seven years before you make your perpetual or final vows.

Pat Kenny: But there must be pressure to stay even if you aren't happy?

Marion: Yes, that's true. Once you join up it's difficult to leave. You become institutionalised. You're afraid to let go of the security.

Pat Kenny: As you would in a prison.

Marion: And just like in prison, we were never free to choose what to do by day or by night. Everything was timetabled and prescribed by the Holy Rule.

Pat Kenny: I must ask you again. Blame?

Marion: Where do I begin! No. Life's a series of decisions! People change. I've changed.

Pat Kenny: Anger?

Marion: Any amount! Tons of it! But having had breast cancer has taught me many a lesson. You can't survive with anger in your heart.

Pat Kenny: Marion, in the book you talk about that priest who harassed and abused you when you went to Sicily on holiday to recover from your breast cancer. Can I ask you about that incident?

Marion: I wrote the book as therapy. It was my way of coping. I have changed some of the names of the nuns. But, yes, I included certain issues because they still bug me. It worries me that I don't know if that priest is still out there in the same position of authority. He has never apologised and the powers that be, both in the Order and in the Catholic Church in England, in my opinion did not deal with this matter properly.

Pat Kenny: But Christian charity? Forgive and forget?

Marion: No. Justice must be done. I think the Catholic Church will do anything to stop getting embroiled in issues to do with sexuality and celibacy. Even priest friends of mine have cut off any contact with me . . . I can only presume they are

377

petrified because they would prefer not to face up to the whole sex thing.

Pat Kenny: So what is it you want to achieve by this book?

Marion: Three letters: SPA.

S equals Sexuality. Get the church to face up to how it regards sexuality.
P equals Pensions for many of my ex-nun friends who have been treated very badly in this regard. Make the Church pay up. Let justice be done!
A equals Anger. I have used writing as a therapy and want to continue to do so.

Pat Kenny: Tell me, do you still have friends in the Order of nuns to which you belonged — the Salesians?

Marion: Yes, I still keep in contact. Although I was treated badly by some — in fact only two, maybe three — of them when I went back to the funeral Mass of a Head Teacher nun who had died.

Pat Kenny: Why? Jealousy? They wished they'd left? Felt you've been disloyal?

Marion: Maybe true for some. But that's no excuse for Sister Rita, who knew me from when I was fourteen, coming to the door and looking straight at me and saying, 'I have no time to talk to you. You can go where you like but don't come near me.' Now she could have been upset at the death of the Sister concerned — she was busy preparing the buffet for the folks returning from the burial — but I was willing to help. I did go in and help but she did not relent and never said she was sorry.

Pat Kenny: Religion! So much for forgiveness and understanding?

Marion: Yes, I've had a glut of it and even though the nuns sent me three invitations to join them in celebrating their centenary of being in this country I don't particularly relish another dose. That goes for going to church too. The fact that I only go to church for funerals and weddings I suppose speaks for itself. And I've discovered that talking to priests and bishops in the Catholic Church is like battering your head gainst a metre-thick stone wall. It's *you* that will suffer. That's what a friend advised when she intimated that I was destroying myself by writing and phoning members of the Salesian Order about the sexual harassment I had experienced in Sicily. Having had cancer, I realise that the anger I have built up inside me is putting me at risk of suffering another bout of the disease and yet I seem unable to let go of the sense of injustice I am experiencing.

Pat Kenny: Do you still try to help others?

Marion: Well, I try to. After I had cancer I became involved with The Fountain Centre in The Royal Surrey Hospital which is a haven for cancer patients. 'Every hospital should have one!' is their slogan. It's a therapeutic centre for cancer patients manned mainly by volunteers. Charlotte and Gail who manage it were there for me and I want them to be there for others.

Pat Kenny: So is there anyone else who really helped you on your way?

Marion: My brother Des. He encouraged me to enter my short story about the Sicily incident in a *Richard and Judy* Competition.

Pat Kenny: I can see from your CV that you didn't win?

Marion: I didn't enter! I wrote my book instead. But, yes, had it not been for my brother Des I would never have made it on to a show for celebrities. Am I one?

Did you miss that chat show? I wore a silk purple suit with cropped trousers and a frilly top.

It was only screened in my dreams.

'*Puro e disposto a salire alle stelle . . .* '
(Pure and ready to mount to the stars . . .)
                    Divina Commedia, Purgatorio,
                    Canto 33 I, 145

                    ★ ★ ★

Marion Dante
On the Feast of Saint John Bosco
31st January 2007

Other titles published by
The House of Ulverscroft:

THE NEWSAGENT'S WINDOW

John Osborne

Moving into an unfurnished house, John uses the ads in newsagents' windows to buy things like a bed and a settee. On impulse, one day, he replies to an advert for a psychic masseur named Lucy, who tells him some home truths. So begins a year of self-discovery and an obsession with newsagents' windows, taking John to a shoe-exhibition, an Ayckbourn play, to a wrestling match. He becomes the owner of a man's entire video collection, a clapped-out Ford Escort — and discovers a community of a bygone age. Looking to improve his German, he meets a pretty German girl named Leni . . .

DEWEY'S NINE LIVES

Vicki Myron with Bret Witter

Vicki Myron described in her first book, *Dewey*, how an abandoned stray became the library cat, and how he transformed many people's lives. His fame spread and his influence transformed a community and touched the world . . . In *Dewey's Nine Lives*, Vicki has included new tales of Dewey, and told of how many of her experiences in recent years were filled with his spirit — especially when two new 'stray cats' entered her world. Also, having met thousands of his fans, she has here collected some of their own heartfelt cat stories — each one resonating with the echoes of Dewey.

WE ARE SOLDIERS

Danny Danziger

Danny Danziger interviews the men and women who fight our wars, giving us an insight into the reality of what we ask of our armed forces. Through these soldiers' eyes, the reader will be taken on training exercises in the jungles of Borneo and the Arctic tundra; enter the Muslim compound of Gorazde as the Serbians fire on children making their way to school; sit in on negotiations with Afghan warlords; learn what troops ask the Regimental Padre as they stand on the front line, and discover what it's like to experience the intense heat of battle.

CONFESSIONS OF A WEDDING PLANNER

Tamryn Kirby

Tamryn Kirby was one of the UK's leading wedding planners, responsible for the most important day of a woman's life. In *Confessions Of A Wedding Planner* Tamryn tells us the funny, sad and sometimes shocking truth about what goes on in pursuit of the perfect day. She's seen it all: The terminally ill bride who defied the odds and walked down the aisle; the mother-in-law who turned up in her own version of the bridal gown; the celebrity who spent her big day planning the 'divorce party', and the groom who called off the wedding as he was taking his vows . . .

THE TEMPTRESS

Paul Spicer

Kenya, 1941. Josslyn Hay, Earl of Erroll, one of the privileged colonial set who farmed their estates in 'Happy Valley', was shot dead in his car. The mystery of who killed him remains unsolved — until now. American heiress Alice de Janze had long been conducting an affair with Joss. However, in her forties, rejected and isolated, Alice committed an act of reckless desperation — resulting in Joss's murder and her own demise. The 'White Mischief' mystery has fascinated film-makers and historians for decades. Paul Spicer's investigation solves the murder of Josslyn Hay and paints a portrait of a dangerous, captivating woman.

A PASSION FOR LIVING

Alexander Stobbs

Our lives are precious. Never more so than for nineteen-year-old Alexander Stobbs. Living with cystic fibrosis, each day could be his last: eating, sleeping and even breathing can be a struggle. His determination to live life to the full is set against the exhausting everyday rigours of medication and treatment to keep him alive. An Eton scholar, who won a music scholarship to King's College Cambridge, his story spurs us to make every day count. Alex takes us on his journey, where, determined to live his dreams, he prepares to conduct Bach's three-hour-long St Matthew Passion . . .